I'VE TAKEN A PAGE IN THE BIBLE!

I'VE TAKEN A PAGE IN THE BIBLE!

A Medley of Jewish Humour

compiled by

Alfred Marks

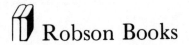 Robson Books

First published in the United Kingdom in
1985 by Robson Books Ltd., Bolsover House,
5-6 Clipstone Street, London W1P 7EB.
© 1985 Alfred Marks.

British Library Cataloguing in Publication Data

I've taken a page in the Bible: a medley of
  Jewish humour.
  1. Jews—Anecdotes, facetiae, etc.
  I. Marks, Alfred
  909'.049240828'0207   DS112

  ISBN 0-86051-348-3

Printed in the United Kingdom by St Edmundsbury Press,
Bury St Edmunds, Suffolk.

CONTENTS

5

It was the time of the Exodus. Moses was leading the tribes out of Egypt when they came to the shore of the Red Sea. On the far side lay the Promised Land and, raising his staff, Moses performed the miracle of parting the waters to freedom.

'Cross,' he said to the leader of the first tribe.

'No,' he replied, shrugging his shoulders.

'What do you mean "no"?'

'I don't want to cross.'

'But I've just performed a miracle... I've parted the Red Sea. You have to cross.'

'Why?'

'Over there's the land of milk and honey... now cross.'

'No.'

'Look,' said Moses, 'you've got to cross. I've taken a page in the Bible.'

FOREWORD

This book isn't so much a book of Jewish jokes as a collection of Jewish humour — but what is humour? What is Jewish humour?

Here you will find work by Jewish humourists, standard Jewish stories and some of my own favourites. 'Standard' is an important word in this context, because Yiddish is probably the only successful Esperanto today, allowing Jews from China (and funny that they don't look it) to communicate with Jews from Afghanistan (and they certainly don't look it) in a common language. That is not to say that what follows is necessarily Yiddish humour. Jewish humour is peculiar in that it has its roots in every country in which the Diaspora (dispersion) has happened. Jews from Russia tell Russian Jewish stories; Jews from England tell English Jewish stories; from America, American Jewish stories — and yet there is a common thread: the philosophy of the Jew.

How have Jews survived through successions of fallen empires and persecutions? Many people have said that humour has kept them going — the ability to laugh at themselves. Many nations claim to have this sort of humour, but it's more pronounced among Jews and is more readily discernible in the stories and jokes they tell.

The Jew will also accept black humour far more readily than many other nationalities do. There are stories from the darkest periods in Jewish history, the holocaust and Russian pogroms, that illustrate this.

There are stereotypes and there are typicals. What, for example, is a typical English joke? Let me offer an example of my own, told to me by the great Leslie Henson. I have deliberately tried telling this story in America, as an example

9

of typical English humour, and it has been greeted with stony silence. Now, it may not be a story that makes you laugh out loud immediately, but in true English fashion, it makes me chuckle to myself when I picture the scene.

Two retired generals met in the Athenaeum and one said to the other, 'How are you, Charles?'

'Well, I've not been too well, old boy — to be honest with you, Algernon, I've been pretty poorly. I went to see my quack and after a while he recommended a visit to one of these psychiatric wallahs. I went along to Wimpole Street. I saw this psychiatric chap. I paid him twenty-five guineas. He laid me on the settee, spoke to me for half an hour and told me I was in love with my umbrella.

'In love with my... I mean, fond of it — yes.'

To me that typifies so much that is English.

And for a typical Jewish story — as opposed to a stereotype? Here is one that portrays a lot of the philosophy of the Jews, as well as their resignation and their logical illogicality:

An English Jew leaves London as a young man, goes to America, and makes his fortune. After thirty years his immediate family in England have all passed away except for his old grandmother, who is still alive in the East End of London. So he decides to pay her a final visit before she dies.

Like all modern Jews he has assimilated and become very American, which takes his grandmother slightly by surprise when he arrives at her little home with a very blonde and obviously non-Jewish wife. However, she welcomes them warmly and in the evening looks forward to a heart-to-heart with her grandson.

'Well, Schmoolik...' she began.

'If you don't mind, grandma, it's not Shmoolik. I changed my name. It's now Sam. You understand?'

'Oh, certainly. I understand. Yes... perfectly. Sam in America. You don't call yourself Shmoolik, you call yourself Sam. This wife — she's not Jewish?'

'No grandma... it's not the thing, you see. People don't mind any more. There's a lot of inter-marriage, a lot of inter-mixing. You understand?'

'Certainly I understand. Of course I understand.... Tell me, do you still go to synagogue on Saturday?'

He paused. 'Well, grandma, you understand, it's very difficult because I'm in business in New York and you can't say to a business associate, "I'm sorry, I can't meet you Saturday — I have to go to temple." You understand?'

'Certainly I understand. Of course I understand.... By the way, you still eat kosher food?'

'Well, grandma, it's very difficult. When you're meeting a business associate, you can't say, "We've got to go to a kosher restaurant." If they say Chinese, you go Chinese; if they say Japanese, you go Japanese; Greek, you go Greek. In business... you understand?'

'Certainly I understand. Of course I understand.... Well, goodnight, Sam.' She walked towards the door and then stopped to ask anxiously, 'You still circumcised, Sam?'

That says a great deal about Jews and Jewish humour.

I hope that in dipping into this book a fuller picture will emerge of what has amused the Jews since the time of Moses and the first readers of the Bible. I have sub-divided the material under very general headings, concluding with a section that seems to me to wrap up the principal theme present in Jewish humour — one that I touch on throughout the book. Many of the stories will have a familiar ring — but that is just one of the many joys of Jewish humour. Like the

11

scholarly writing in the Talmud (of which more a little later) these tales have been chewed over and reworked by countless Jewish humourists for centuries. What you will find here are my favourite versions complemented by a few extracts of longer pieces of humorous writing which expand the broad themes touched on in each section.

You Should Laugh So Long

A tradition of Jewish humour

One of the riches of Jewish humour is its heritage, lying deeply rooted in a folklore that stretches back to the beginnings of recorded history. Don't ask me what humour is — I'm only a comedian after all. But with Jewish humour there are clearly defined characteristics that crop up throughout the centuries, shaped and moulded by the conditions of their period, but timeless in the fundamental image they portray. These don't provide a definition of humour, but they act as pointers and clues to coming to a closer appreciation and understanding of it.

Characterization is one of the great strengths of Jewish humour; shrewd but good-humoured observation of those human traits that distinguish the individual from the anonymous crowd. Jewish humour is populated by dozens of 'stock' characters that evolved in the millennia of Jewish history and many of them feature in one guise or another in the stories and anecdotes in this book. To begin with, I have selected four groups that epitomize well known qualities attributed to the Jew, the first of which is an entire community — the people of Chelm.

Chelm is a mythological town peopled by fools. It is the birthplace of every stupid Jewish story, a community that staggers from one non-sequitur to the next, from where anyone with a grain of sense has long since departed.

No doubt there is a similar community in Ireland. There is probably one in Poland, too. And doubtless they too indulge in the same painstaking reasoning and logic (or illogicality — but I am jumping the gun) that permeates every Chelm story and lends it its peculiar charm and unique wisdom.

One night a fire broke out in the main schoolhouse in Chelm. Luckily, all the inhabitants rallied round, and eventually managed to put the fire out, though not before it had done considerable damage. After pausing a while to allow the crowd to draw breath, the rabbi began to address them.

'Fellow citizens of Chelm,' he cried, 'can you not see that this fire was a present sent to us from God Himself?'

The crowd were surprised, and many of them shook their heads in disbelief.

'Look at it this way,' the rabbi explained. 'If it were not for the light provided by the bright flames, how would we have been able to put the fire out on such a dark night?'

*   *   *   *   *

The old men of Chelm were discussing what they'd do if they had a lot of money, like the wealthy Zalman from the nearby town of Purim.

'The thing is,' said the first man, 'if I were Zalman, I'd be even richer than he is.'

'How is that possible?' questioned his friend. 'If you were Zalman, you'd both have exactly the same amount of money.'

'Not so,' replied the first man. 'You see, I'd do a little teaching on the side!'

*   *   *   *   *

A merchant from Chelm began a journey lasting several weeks by spending a few days in a neighbouring town dealing with some business there. On his first night he unpacked his clothes and found that he had left his slippers at home. So the next morning he sent a message back to Chelm addressed to his wife. 'Please send me your slippers,' it began. 'I have written "your slippers", because I know that if I had written "my slippers" you would have read it as "my slippers" and would have sent me your slippers. What use would your slippers be to me? That's why I was careful to write "your slippers" so that you would read "your slippers" and send me my slippers.'

        *   *   *   *   *

Two of the wisest men in Chelm were locked in an intricate argument. 'What I want to know is why the Czar has to collect a rouble from me in taxes when he can make as many roubles as he likes in the mint,' commented one of them.

'That's a ridiculous question,' said the other. 'Just look at the Jew: every time he does a good deed, he creates an angel. Following your argument, you might as well ask: why does God need a Jew's good deed just to add his angel to the millions and millions in heaven? Isn't he able to create as many as He likes? Yes He is, so why doesn't He? Simply because he prefers *your* angel. The same goes for the taxes. Of course the Czar can make as many roubles as he likes; but he prefers *your* rouble, that's all.'

        *   *   *   *   *

The rabbi of Chelm held a surgery each evening, where he would offer to sort out any of the villagers' problems. At just such a surgery one evening, Aaron the baker came to see the rabbi about an experience which had been bothering him for some days.

17

'It was the most extraordinary thing,' began Aaron. 'You would agree, rabbi, that whenever a poor man such as I drops a piece of bread, it never fails to land butter-side down.'

'Yes, that is invariably the case,' nodded the rabbi.

'Well, a few days ago, I dropped my bread, and it landed butter-side up!' exclaimed Aaron.

'Impossible,' cried the rabbi. 'This has never happened before.'

'I assure you, rabbi, it did happen. I swear it on my mother's life!'

The rabbi pondered the situation for a few moments, and then turned to the baker with a smile on his face. 'I have it, my son!' he explained. 'You must have buttered your bread on the wrong side.'

*　　*　　*　　*　　*

The rabbi from Chelm went on a visit to Pinsk. While he was at the synagogue there he got into conversation with the *shamus*, the caretaker who comes at the bottom of the pecking order after the rabbi and cantor in any synagogue.

Realizing that he now had the chance to get the better of at least one rabbi, the *shamus* asked the visitor from Chelm if he liked riddles.

'Of course. Who doesn't?' the rabbi answered.

'Right, try this one,' said the *shamus*. 'Who is my mother's son, but not my brother?'

The rabbi from Chelm had met his match. No matter how he turned this round in his mind he couldn't fathom who could be this man's mother's son but not his brother. 'I give up,' he finally admitted. 'Who is your mother's son, but not your brother?'

'*I* am!' the *shamus* told him gleefully.

The rabbi from Chelm was delighted with this. He couldn't wait to get home to try it on the good people of the

18

town, and as soon as he was back he called them together and asked, 'Who is my mother's son, but not my brother?'

Well, if the rabbi from Chelm couldn't puzzle it out, there wasn't much hope for anyone else. Everyone had a good try though, and puzzled over the riddle all morning until — one by one — they admitted defeat and asked the rabbi for the answer.

The mayor, acting as spokesman for the town, eventually asked, 'Tell us, rabbi, who is your mother's son but not your brother?'

Smiling at them indulgently, the rabbi answered. 'The *shamus* from Pinsk, of course.'

*   *   *   *   *

The rabbi from Chelm was disturbed early one morning by a young man whose wife had just given birth.

'Rabbi,' he shouted as he reached the door, 'something extraordinary happened. My wife has just had a baby and you know we have only been married three months. How can this happen?'

The rabbi was a man of the world and took the young man into his study. 'My son,' he began, 'let me ask you something. Have you or have you not lived with your wife for three months?'

'I have.'

'And has she or has she not lived with you for three months?'

'She has.'

'And have you not lived together for three months?'

'We have.'

'What is the total then — three months plus three months plus three?'

'Nine months!'

'That's right. So why do you bother me with your silly questions?'

'This is a wonderful horse!' exclaimed a horse dealer on a visit to Chelm, when one of the citizens showed more than passing interest in the animal. 'It gallops so fast,' he went on, 'that if you set out from Chelm at two in the morning you'd be in Lublin by five!'

The prospective purchaser looked doubtful. 'What on earth do you expect me to do in Lublin at that hour in the morning?' he asked.

*   *   *   *   *

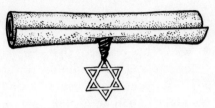

One of the most ubiquitous characters in Jewish humour is the schnorrer. *Translated literally, this means a 'beggar', though the meaning runs far deeper than that. The* schnorrer *is a beggar with* chutzpah, *with cheek. He is the sort of beggar who will come up to you in the street and ask, 'Can you give me a pound for a coffee?', and when you tell him a coffee only costs fifty pence, answers, 'I know, but I like to tip big.'*

The schnorrer *is no simpleton. He would run rings round the 'wise men' of Chelm and he uses his intelligence and guile to perfect his begging to a fine art that enables him brazenly to extract money by playing on the Jewish sense of preservation.*

A rich furrier was woken up at six o'clock one Sunday morning by the sound of someone banging on his door. When he got downstairs, and opened the door, he found one of the local *schnorrers* standing there asking him for money. ·

He immediately lost his temper. 'What the hell do you think you're doing waking me at this time in the morning?'

'My dear sir,' said the *schnorrer* calmly. 'I do not tell you how to run your fur business, please don't tell me how to run mine!'

*   *   *   *   *

I've Taken a Page in the Bible

As Mr Baumgarten was leaving the synagogue, he was stopped by a *schnorrer*. He was just about to give the poor man some money when he realized that he had seen him somewhere before. 'Hang on a minute, you scoundrel,' he yelled accusingly, 'I distinctly remember seeing you begging outside the Catholic church across the road only yesterday. Now you're begging outside the synagogue. Make up your mind, you damned swindler! Are you a Catholic or a Jew?'

'A Jew, a Jew,' admitted the *schnorrer*, shrugging his shoulders. 'But be reasonable, sir — who can make a good living out of only one religion these days?'

* * * * *

A *schnorrer* knocked at a door and asked for alms, only to be told by the man who answered the door, 'I don't have a cent in the house. Why don't you call back tomorrow?'

'My friend,' said the *schnorrer*, standing his ground, 'if only you knew the fortune I have lost by giving credit.'

* * * * *

A wealthy Jew, who for many years had supported the same *schnorrer* with generous annual donations, sent him only half the usual amount on one occasion, which raised a loud complaint from the recipient.

'I'm sorry,' said his benefactor. 'The truth is I have had huge expenses this year with my eldest daughter getting married. The wedding alone cost me a fortune, not to mention all the other costs involved.'

'What's that got to do with me?' enquired the *schnorrer* indignantly. 'Next time you decide to marry off one of your daughters, I'd be grateful if you did it with your own money — not mine!'

* * * * *

A rich Jew who came across a *schnorrer* looking half-starved and holding out his hands to passers-by gave him a dollar and told to go and buy something to eat. A couple of hours later he entered his own lunch-time haunt and was infuriated to find the same *schnorrer* sitting down at a table and tucking into a roll topped with smoked salmon.

'I call it a damn cheek,' said the rich man, going up to the *schnorrer*. 'You beg money on the street. I give you a dollar so you can go buy something to eat and what do I find — you're sitting here stuffing yourself on *bagel* and *lox*!'

'And why not?' asked the *schnorrer*, after wiping his lips with the napkin. 'Before I got your dollar I couldn't eat *bagel* and *lox*. Now I have it, I mustn't eat *bagel* and *lox*. In that case would you mind telling me when I *am* supposed to eat *bagel* and *lox*?'

*   *   *   *   *

A *schnorrer* came to see the famous banker Rothschild one day. 'Please help me,' he begged. 'My life has been one long bad luck story from beginning to end!'

'Tell me a little about yourself,' enquired Rothschild. 'What do you do for a living?'

'What *did* I do, more like. I trained for many years to become a professional musician, and the first orchestra I joined closed down after two months. Now I can't get any work!'

'That's bad luck,' agreed Rothschild. 'And what instrument do you play?'

'The French horn.'

'The French horn! You're kidding?' cried the delighted Baron. 'It's my favourite instrument. In fact, I've got one of my own. Don't worry, my friend, I'll help you out with some money, but first, you must show me how well you play the French horn.'

The *schnorrer* sighed deeply, and buried his face in his

23

hands. 'What did I tell you about my bad luck!' he wailed. 'Of all the instruments in the orchestra, I had to go and pick the French horn!'

*   *   *   *   *

Two shabbily-dressed *schnorrers* were passing a few hours in a cemetery one afternoon, when they suddenly spotted a huge, expensively-decorated mausoleum.

'My God!' said the first *schnorrer* in amazement. 'It's made of pure marble, and engraved with gold!'

'You know whose it is, don't you?' asked the second *schnorrer*. 'It belongs to the Rothschilds!'

'You don't say,' replied the first *schnorrer*. 'Those guys certainly know how to live!'

*   *   *   *   *

A *schnorrer* was standing outside the house of Brodsky, the millionaire, waiting for his companion, when he noticed him being physically ejected from the front door.

'What happened?' he asked his friend.

'They chucked me out for insolence, but I think it's something else.'

'What do you mean?'

'Well, as I was standing in the hall, I peered into the music room, and you know what I saw?'

'No, what?'

'Two girls playing the same piano! If you ask me, this guy Brodsky's got a few money troubles!'

*   *   *   *   *

A small, scruffily-dressed old man, wearing dark glasses and carrying a white stick, was standing in a doorway looking dejected. When a elderly woman happened to walk past, the man began to wail: 'Help a poor, blind Jew! Help a poor, blind Jew!'

The woman immediately stopped, and dropped a five-dollar note into his outstretched hand, saying, 'May God have pity on you, you unfortunate soul.'

'Thank you, madam,' cried the *schnorrer*, gratefully. 'The minute I saw you, I knew you had a generous spirit!'

* * * * *

In contrast to the schnorrer, *who is a past master at seizing the smallest opportunity and exploiting it, comes the* schlemiel, *the dolt. When he seizes an opportunity it bites him. When he takes a plunge the pool is empty. It doesn't matter what he turns his hand to, somehow he always manages to get things wrong. Generals who manage to snatch defeat from the jaws of victory are* schlemiels, *so are those heroes who throw lifelines to drowning men, but forget to hang on to one end!*

One *schlemiel* fell on such hard times that he was reduced to asking for help from the town council. They seemed reluctant to advance a single kopeck and in desperation the *schlemiel* told them, 'If you won't help me — I'll become a hat-maker!'

They all laughed at this, and one of the council asked, 'So what? Go and be a hat-maker.'

'But, don't you understand? With my luck, the moment I go into the hat business every baby born in this town will come into the world without a head!'

*   *   *   *   *

A scholar, who was admired by the rest of the world for his learning and wisdom, was still only a *schlemiel* in the eyes of his wife because he was always losing things.

One afternoon he came from the Turkish bath absorbed in thought, quite oblivious to the fact that he wasn't wearing a shirt.

'And what have you done with your shirt?' his wife asked with weary resignation.

'The shirt? I suppose someone must have picked up mine in mistake for his own.'

'In that case, where is his? I can see perfectly well that you haven't got your own.'

'I can't think,' said the scholar, scratching his beard. 'He must have been careless, he forgot to leave me that!'

* * * * *

One of the hazards of many *schlemiels* was being henpecked. One poor man found himself used as example by his wife when several of her friends came to visit her one afternoon.

'*Schlemiel*,' she yelled at him, 'get under that table this minute.'

Obediently, he scuttled under the table — to his wife's obvious pleasure and the delight of her friends.

'Now, come out!' she shouted.

'No, I won't!' he shouted back, trying to sound defiant. 'I'll show you who's still master in this house.'

* * * * *

One night a *schlemiel* was woken by a burglar sneaking into his impoverished home. As soon as he realized he had disturbed someone in the tiny house, the burglar tried to get away — but the *schlemiel* caught him, saying excitedly, 'No, no, please don't go yet. Let me help you look around. Maybe your luck will be better than mine.'

27

A powerful government official summoned a *schlemiel* to his house one day and told him to go to the market in the next town to buy a French poodle for his wife. The *schlemiel* saw a way to make a little on the side and asked how much the official was prepared to pay.

'I'll go up to twenty roubles,' he replied.

'Twenty roubles!' said the *schlemiel* in astonishment. 'Surely you know that you'll be lucky to find a really first-class French poodle for three times that amount.'

The official looked doubtful, and argued that from what he'd heard twenty roubles was a very fair price. But the *schlemiel* argued so convincingly that it was sixty or nothing, that he eventually handed over the sixty roubles and told the *schlemiel* to be as quick as he could.

'Of course, of course,' he replied, sounding just a little uncertain. 'By the way, your Excellency, what exactly is a French poodle?'

*　　*　　*　　*　　*

When all else had failed, *schemiel* went to his rabbi for advice. 'Tell me, what ought I to do?' he implored. 'It doesn't matter what I try, it always ends in disaster. I try selling umbrellas — the rain stops. I try being an undertaker — people stop dying. What work *can* I do?'

'Try being a baker,' suggested the rabbi. 'Bakers always have bread in the house.'

'You've got a point there... but suppose I run out of money to buy the flour, what then?'

'Then you won't be a baker any more,' said the rabbi dismissively.

*　　*　　*　　*　　*

A small town in Lithuania was swept by fire one night and the scene of devastation that greeted the townspeople at dawn prompted the town treasurer to open the municipal coffers to give aid to the victims. Among those queueing was a poor *schlemiel* whose little house had been one of the very few to escape the blaze.

'What are you doing here?' asked the treasurer angrily. 'Do you mean to tell me that you suffered in the fire!'

'Did I suffer! It scared me to death!'

*   *   *   *   *

'What's up with you?' the miller asked the *schlemiel* of a *bagel* baker when he delivered his regular consignment of flour.

'Business is bad,' answered the baker. 'Bagels are going to be the ruin of me yet.'

'Why, what's the matter with *bagels*?'

'There's no profit in them. If I make the hole big, look how much flour has to go into the dough to go round that hole.'

'So, what's the problem? Make the hole smaller.'

'All right, so I make the hole smaller. But look how much flour has to go into the dough to fill the *bagel*.'

*   *   *   *   *

When Freed, the wealthy milliner, died, a lot of people attended his funeral. Throughout the town he was known as a good and generous man and many in the crowd following the hearse were in tears. One man in particular, a *schlemiel*, was very distressed and sobbed uncontrollably.

'Are you a close relative?' asked the man walking next to him.

'No,' wailed the man in tears.

'Perhaps you were a good friend?'

'No, I never knew the man.'

'Then why are you so upset?'

'That's why!'

29

*The fourth group of 'stock' characters I want to touch on
combines both the spiritual and secular sides of Jewish life,
and in so doing links the wild illogicality of so much Jewish
humour with the down-to-earth business of making a living
and advancing yourself. These are the marriage brokers or*
shadchen, *the men who used to perform (and in ultra-
orthodox communities still do perform) the role of arranging
marriages, even among the most unlikely partners.*

The shadchen *combines many qualities found in
Jewish humour. Hope, despair, opportunism and wild
flights of impossible ambition are equally at home in his
personality, not to mention the intense interest in people,
their affairs (of every description) and what makes them
tick.*

After several attempts to find a wife for a particularly
unprepossessing young man the resourceful *shadchen* tried a
final ploy. Taking the boy's father aside he said to him,
'Listen, there may be a girl lined up for your Simon after all.
She's got a hundred thousand pounds.'

'Great!' said the father. 'Can we see a photograph?'

'For a hundred thousand pounds you want to see a
photograph?'

*   *   *   *   *

30

A young man was listening to the *shadchen* list the wonderful attributes of the prospective bride. When at last the *shadchen* seemed to have finished, the young man said, wryly, 'And what about the limp?'

'What?' asked the *shadchen*, professing surprise.

'She limps,' said the young man.

'Only when she walks!'

*   *   *   *   *

A *shadchen* had been bargaining with Yoshke for weeks. He just couldn't seem to convince him that he had found the girl of his dreams.

'Look,' said Yoshke finally, 'before I make my final decision, I have one request to make.'

'Anything,' said the broker.

'I want to see her in the nude.'

'Out of the question,' shouted the outraged *shadchen*. 'What do you take her for — she's a nice Jewish girl.'

'I'm sorry,' insisted Yoshke. 'No nudity, no deal.'

'*Oy veh*,' cried the broker in desperation, 'if you insist!'

So he went to see the young lady in question, and explained the situation. After many strong objections, and much soul-searching, the girl finally agreed to the strange request. The next day, the *shadchen* went to Yoshke, certain that he would now complete the deal. 'So, did you find her satisfactory?'

'No,' replied Yoshke. 'I can't stand her nose!'

*   *   *   *   *

A *shadchen* went up to a man for whom he was trying to find a wife and said, 'I've got a girl I want you to meet, but for God's sake don't open your mouth. Leave it to me to do the talking, because one of the arts of being a good *shadchen* is to exaggerate to sell you.'

So he took the very plain boy to meet the girl and her

family. They all sat formally round the table drinking a drop of home-made wine and eating a little biscuit.

'Does he earn much?' asked the prospective father-in-law.

'Much?!' asked the *shadchen*, 'Much! He earns thirty roubles a week.'

'Is he kind?'

'Kind?! He looks after sick animals, he's so kind.'

'Is he young?'

'Is he young?! He may look thirty-five, but he's only twenty.'

When he said that the prospective bride-groom coughed.

'Has he got a cough?' asked the girl's father.

'Cough?! Galloping consumption!'

*　　*　　*　　*　　*

A struggling young artist was bemoaning his lack of success with women to the local *shadchen*.

'I just can't seem to find anyone who is sensitive enough to my needs as an artist,' he complained.

'Don't worry, my son,' reassured the *shadchen*. 'I think I know just the girl for a creative soul like you.'

When the *shadchen* arrived at the artist's house the following day with the girl, the artist was amazed at her ugliness, and immediately took the broker to one side.

'Have you gone mad?' he yelled. 'She's a monster! One eye's bigger than the other, her forehead's bigger than her face, and her nose is squashed to one side!'

'Call yourself an artist!' scoffed the *shadchen*. 'Don't you know you've got to live with a Picasso to appreciate it?'

*　　*　　*　　*　　*

A *shadchen* was having great difficulty persuading the young man of the suitability of his prospective in-laws. So he suggested that they went and took tea with them. As they left, it was obvious that the young man was still not fully convinced.

'I don't trust them,' he said. 'I don't think they're half as wealthy as you make them out to be.'

'What do you mean?' replied the *shadchen*. 'You saw for yourself that they had lovely silverware, and real china, and an expensive tablecloth.'

'They could easily have borrowed all those things to impress me,' challenged the suspicious young man.

'Impossible,' snapped the *shadchen*, forgetting himself for a moment. 'Do you think anyone would lend anything valuable to those people!'

*   *   *   *   *

Every community has its *shadchen*, and there was no doubting that Avrum Rabinowitch was one of the wiliest on his part of the coast. He had arranged more marriages than there are stars in the sky. One morning, as he was taking his daily constitutional along the beach, a very strange thing happened. Something began to stir just below the surface of the waves.

Suddenly, an enormous three-headed beast reared up out of the water. It was a truly horrible sight, covered in green slime, and its skin was pitted with hundreds of small craters. Not surprisingly, Avrum's first reaction was one of stunned silence, but as his fear gradually subsided, a thought occurred to him. He rushed over to the creature from the deep.

'Listen,' he said, with a conspiratorial smile on his face, 'have I got a girl for you!'

*   *   *   *   *

Morris was an unattractive youth, and his father began to despair of ever getting him married. In the end he engaged the services of a *shadchen*. After a preliminary consultation the

33

shadchen said, 'Well, I have in mind the very girl for young Morris — Princess Anne, Queen Elizabeth of England's daughter.' (This was before the Princess had met and married Captain Mark Phillips, naturally.)

Morris's father was aghast. 'A *shikseh?*' he said. 'Are you suggesting my Morris should marry a girl who isn't Jewish?'

'Why the prejudice? It's a good family,' soothed the *shadchen.*

'Well, the boy's grandmother will never accept a girl who isn't a Jew,' the father said. 'She's very pious and set in her ways.'

'I'll talk to her,' said the *shadchen,* and he went off to see the old woman. It wasn't easy. There were tears, reproaches, recriminations; a scene that lasted most of the day until everyone was exhausted. The old lady held out well, but in the end, because of her advanced years, she yielded, on the understanding that Princess Anne was a good girl from a fine family and the children would be brought up as Jews.

The *shadchen* and Morris's father left utterly drained. 'So,' said the *shadchen* with a weary smile, 'the rest is easy.'

*   *   *   *   *

Soon after the Russian revolution a *shadchen* paid a visit to one of his lady clients who'd decided the time had come to get married.

'How much dowry do you have?' he asked casually.

'A couple of thousand roubles.'

'A couple of thousand roubles,' repeated the *shadchen,* taking out his client book and flicking through the pages. 'Well, for that I can offer you a doctor.'

'No... I don't want a doctor.'

'How about a rabbi, then?'

'No, not a rabbi.'

'Well, would a cantor suit you? You could get to like his singing.'

'No. That's not what I want either. I want a worker. That's what I'd really like.'

'A worker? That's a good one!' said the *shadchen*. 'For a couple of thousand roubles you think you can get a worker?'

*   *   *   *   *

The tradition of taking favourite themes and reworking them into new stories is still widespread in Jewish humour and among the most entertaining of contemporary story-tellers is David Kossoff, whose collection of tales about his rabbi Mark, A Small Town is a World, *contains this delightful example of the working of the Jewish mind.*

In the twenty-five years that Mark had been the Rabbi in the little town of Klaneshtetl he had learnt far more than he had taught — and knew it. His parishioners were a very mixed bunch and needed a lot of patience and skill. They could be very irritating indeed. 'Not all of them,' Mark would say to Sophie. 'Not the young and the old. It's the middle lot.'

For the very old Mark had special affection, for the dozen or so old men who were in the little synagogue every morning for the early service and who stayed on to discuss things, to argue, to doze off near the stove. 'My Temple Elders,' Mark would call them, and when he could spare time he would stay on with them, just to listen, and chuckle.

This morning, a chilly morning of sudden showers, old Fyvel had arrived late, holding things up, for a quorum was needed before a service could start and he was the tenth. He'd come in soaked, umbella in hand.

'Why didn't you use your umbrella?' Mark asked, concerned.

'I did. I did,' said Fyvel. 'It's old, full of holes.'

'Why did you have it with you?' said Mark.

'I didn't think it would rain,' said Fyvel.

The other Elders had nodded in perfect understanding. They put Fyvel by the stove to dry and began the service. After, they stayed. It was cosy and also there were things to talk about. In particular the matter of the stolen poor-box. Thief unknown and no clues, not that the old men wanted to catch and punish. To replace was more important, so that charity and the giving of alms should not be interrupted.

'The new box is ready,' announced Potchik, who was nearly the eldest, and a respected voice. 'But this time we will fix it to the ceiling, where no robber can reach it. A good solution, yes?'

The wisdom was applauded. 'How,' asked old Fyvel, with steam still rising from him, 'how, if the box is on the ceiling, will people be able to put money in?'

A good point. It was considered carefully, old fingers combing through beards.

'A ladder,' proclaimed Potchik at last. 'A ladder, for the use of the charitable. Available at all times. Molik will lend his ladder from his orchard. Eh, Molik?'

Molik nodded. 'But the ladder is old and unsteady,' he said. 'It takes skill. On soft earth, yes. On a level floor, very dangerous. A person could fall. The charitable should not be put at risk. It is not right.'

Here was also wisdom. Again the old heads nodded and gave thought. It was very quiet. Mark waited. These moments for him were beyond price.

This time it was Zelman, the oldest of them all, who spoke. A true sage.

'A new ladder. Of a kind easy to climb and with a handrail. And to avoid risk to the charitable it should be secured strongly to both floor and ceiling.'

There was a feeling of contentment and happiness in the little synagogue. Another problem solved. Ah, the wisdom of old age.

Mark nodded with the Elders, enchanted, in full agreement. He considered whether he should point out something, but decided it could wait.

* * * * *

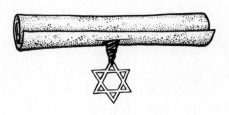

Before moving away from the traditions of Jewish humour into more specific areas I think it is important (not to say entertaining) to glance at some of the lighter sides of the Talmud, *for in that vast canon of scholarship and study some of the principal elements in Jewish humour take their roots.*

At first glance the Talmud *might not seem the most obvious place to search for humorous anecdotes. Running to sixty-three books, it was built up over a thousand years by Jewish scholars writing erudite commentaries on the* Torah *(the first five books of the Bible) and later commenting on the commentaries. The* Talmud *became, therefore, the principal source of all Jewish teaching and doctrine and inevitably it spread its interest to cover both theology and the practical considerations of and applications of the faith. As a result the* Talmud *is packed with observations on every subject under the sun from marriage and beauty to the higher realms of logical deduction.*

Woven into this fabric of Jewish lore are many entertaining examples of the type of misguided reasoning that later come to light in Chelm as well as the rabbinical wisdom which underlies so many Jewish stories.

The extracts I have chosen are taken from Hyam Maccoby's selection from the Talmud, The Day God Laughed.

39

AN OVERSUBTLE ARGUMENT

R abbi Jose ben Taddai of Tiberias put the following *a fortiori* argument to Rabban Gamaliel: I am forbidden to marry my daughter, but my daughter's mother is permitted to me.

All the more so, then, I should be forbidden to marry the daughter of someone who is forbidden to me.

I am forbidden to marry somebody else's wife.

Therefore, I should be forbidden to marry the daughter of somebody else's wife.

Therefore all marriages should be forbidden (except to the daughters of unmarried mothers, widows or divorcees).

For this argument, Rabban Gamaliel excommunicated Rabbi Jose ben Taddai (on the ground he was bringing rabbinical methods of argument into discredit).

BETTER NOT TO BE BORN?

F or two and a half years the House of Shammai and the House of Hillel disputed. The House of Shammai argued that it would have been better for man not to have been created; and the House of Hillel argued that it was better for man to have been created than not to have been created.

In the end, a vote was taken, and it was decided: 'It would have been better for man not to have been created, but now that he has been created, let him scrutinize his deeds.'

THE UGLY WIFE

A certain man said to his wife, 'I vow that you will derive no benefit from me until you show me that there is something beautiful in you.'

He came before Rabbi Ishmael ben Rabbi Yosi, who said to him, 'Perhaps her head is beautifully shaped.'

He said to him, 'No, it is round.'

'Perhaps she has beautiful hair.'

'No, it is like stalks of flax.'

'Perhaps her eyes are beautiful.

'Goggle-eyed.'

'Perhaps her ears are beautiful.'

'They are doubled over.'

'Perhaps her nose is beautiful.'

'It is swollen.'

'Her lips?'

'Thick.'

'Her neck?'

'Sunken.'

'Her belly?'

'Distended.'

'Her legs?'

'She waddles like a goose.'

'Perhaps she has a beautiful name?'

'She is called Muck.'

'The vow is fulfilled. Her name suits her beautifully.'

WERE THE LIONS HUNGRY?

Caesar said to Rabbi Tanhum, 'Come, let us all become one people.'

Said Rabbi Tanhum, 'By my life, we who are circumcised cannot become like you. You, then, should be circumcised and become like us.'

'A very good answer. Unfortunately, however, anyone who defeats the Emperor in an argument must be thrown to the lions.'

So they threw Rabbi Tanhum to the lions. The lions, however, did not eat him.

41

An unbeliever, who was standing by, said. 'The reason why the lions do not eat him is that they are not hungry.'

To test this theory, they threw the unbeliever to the lions, who ate him.

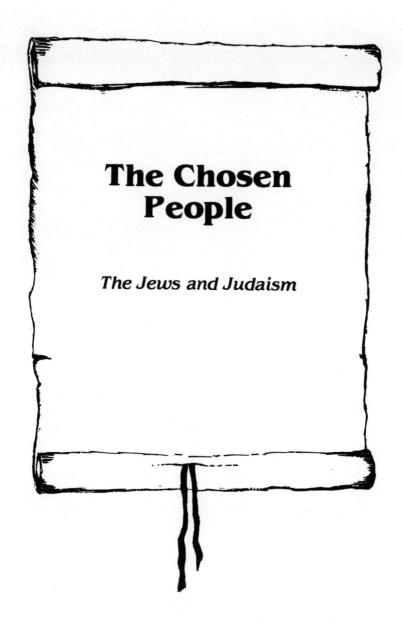

The Chosen People

The Jews and Judaism

'Dear God,' wrote Sholom Aleichem, the great Yiddish writer whose stories about Tevyeh the Dairyman were later adapted to create Fiddler on the Roof, 'I know we are your chosen people, but couldn't you choose some other people for a change?'

Turned in on their own communities as they were for centuries, the Jews have incorporated their religion into almost every strand of life — particularly their humour. Jokes about rabbis, cantors, and sextons abound, and so do many about God!

With so much suffering having been endured in defence of the faith, it has produced a deep-rooted attachment even among those who may not consider themselves particularly devout. This attachment is frequently the focal point of many Jewish stories, where religious observance is often portrayed as the innocent tool of more worldly considerations, especially when status is involved.

The bar mitzvah, the ceremony in which thirteen-year-old boys reach the status and assume the duties of a 'man', is a common setting for stories of one-upmanship, though even in reality they can have their humorous side. Here is Groucho Marx describing his own bar mitzvah:

'I remember my bar mitzvah speech. It was a great speech. My father bought it for five dollars, and all five boys used it. Each of us boys used the same speech. A dollar a man.'

I've Taken a Page in the Bible

He even remembered how it began, as he recalled to his friend Arthur Whitelaw, to whom he was describing the event:

' "My dear parents: For thirteen long years you have toiled and laboured for my happiness. From the moment I saw the light of day you have watched over me . . ." Or "washed over me" — I forget which.'

The humour of the Jews often points up that fact that religious ceremony and many other aspects of their faith can take on more than a spiritual dimension, as the following stories suggest.

———————————————

A certain amount of jealousy separated two guests at a *bar mitzvah* from their hosts. As they were greeted by the proud parents, they surveyed the unashamedly opulent scene with scarcely disguised envy. Choice wines awaited the guests; mouth-watering displays of expensive food tempted their appetites and in the centre stood a life-size sculpture of the *bar mitzvah* boy meticulously created out of chopped liver.

'And what do you think of the statue of my Bernie?' asked the mother enthusiastically.

'I've never seen anything quite like it,' replied one of the guests acidly. 'Who did it? Lipchitz or Epstein?'

'Lipchitz, of course!' replied the mother. 'Epstein only works in egg and onions.'

*　　*　　*　　*　　*

For a time it was the fashion to stage the most lavish *bar mitzvah*s. Parents used to go to extraordinary lengths in organizing these ceremonies for their sons. Some took place on jet aircraft; some on the *QE II*; others in submarines.

One couple were at a loss what to do in the way of one-upmanship until the husband had the idea of arranging a safari in Africa. All the guests were flown out first-class. Fourteen elephants were lined up to transport them. Full tropical kit was provided for everyone, and they set off in a state of absolute euphoria.

After an hour's trek through the jungle, the line of elephants came to a halt, and the father of the *bar mitzvah* boy called for the head guide and asked what the matter was.

'Sorry, *Bwana*, another *bar mitzvah* ahead of us.'

*   *   *   *   *

A rabbi, wishing to impress his humility on those assembled before him, cried out in the middle of a service, 'Oh, Lord, I am nothing!'

The cantor, afraid of being outdone, also cried out, 'Oh, Lord, I am nothing!'

The sexton of the synagogoue, who was duly impressed by these outbursts, cried, 'I, too, am nothing!'

The rabbi turned to the cantor and said, 'Look who thinks he's nothing!'

*   *   *   *   *

The congregation of a wealthy synagogue hired a cantor to sing on the principal holy days and were greatly impressed by the clarity and beauty of his voice.

'I've never heard singing like that,' said one of them to a friend on their way home from service.

'What's so special?' he was asked. 'If I had his voice I could sing as good!'

47

I've Taken a Page in the Bible

At a village meeting in Poland the community's need for a new synagogue was being hotly debated. No one argued that they didn't need it, the problem was how to raise the money. Then one man rose to his feet and suggested, 'We should put a tax on the village prostitutes.'

One indignant learned rabbi stood up and asked, 'Do you honestly suggest that we should use the money from prostitutes to build a synagogue?'

'Why not?' answered the man. 'It's our money.'

*　　*　　*　　*　　*

The American spacemen landed on Mars, a first for mankind. They put on their spacesuits and began to explore the planet. In the distance they could see weird yellow mountains and red water — the sort of landscape seen in science fiction movies. They radioed earth.

'Tom here, Houston. It's a bleak planet with no visible signs of life,' said the astronaut. Suddenly his friend pulled his arm.

'Look over there!'

They looked into the distance and saw what looked like a troop of green men walking towards them. The spacemen were amazed. As the green group got nearer, they were even more shocked to see that each of the group was wearing a long black coat, long sidelocks, a full beard and a Russian fur hat.

'Hello, we're from the planet Earth', said the spaceman. 'Who are you?'

'Us? Ve're Martians!' the green man replied.

'Tell me,' asked the astronaut, 'do they all dress like you here?'

'No,' replied the green man. 'Only the orthodox ones.'

*　　*　　*　　*　　*

An inveterate old atheist was lying on his deathbed, when he suddenly asked his wife to send for the rabbi.

'I want to confess my sins, and do penance,' he gasped.

'But, my dear, aren't you being a little hypocritical? You've always been convinced of the folly of religion. What makes you change your mind now?'

'Don't you see?' said the old man with a twinkle in his eye. 'I want to make a mockery of that old Talmudic dogma: "The wicked do not repent even at the gates of Heaven"!'

*   *   *   *   *

A little boy was sent to *cheder*, the Hebrew school that every boy preparing for *bar mitzvah* has to attend. After he had been going for four weeks his father asked what he was learning. 'We learnt the *kaddish*,' said his son.

'The *kaddish*? But that's the prayer for the dead. Your mother and I are still alive!'

So he stormed up to the rabbi when he next saw him and said, 'What's the idea of teaching my son the *kaddish* when we're both alive?'

'You should live so long till he learns it,' replied the rabbi.

*   *   *   *   *

A Professor at Columbia University asked his graduate students to write a thesis on some aspect of the rabbit. Among his class were several overseas students.

A Japanese student submitted a thesis entitled: 'Rabbits — The Workforce of the Future?'

A French student submitted a thesis entitled: 'The Sex Life of the Rabbit'.

A British student submitted a thesis entitled: 'The Problems of Rabbit Hunting'.

An Indian student submitted a thesis entitled: 'Twenty-five Ways to Curry a Rabbit'.

Leo Schwartz, also a student in the class, submitted a thesis entitled: 'Rabbits and the Jewish Problem'.

*   *   *   *   *

Groucho Marx could always be relied on to introduce the unorthodox into anything with which he was involved. In the collection of reminiscences about him, Hello, I Must Be Going *by Charlotte Chandler, Groucho's friend Arthur Whitelaw recalls going to a* seder, *the religious service celebrated on the first night of the Passover, in Groucho's house:*

I hadn't been to a *seder* for years. If Louis B. Meyer and Irving Thalberg were still alive, it might have been called *A Night at the Seder*. Over there was a dais. Besides me, Elliott Gould, George Segal, actor Warren Berlinger, Groucho's lawyer Ed Pearlstein, and a Mr Schubert were there. I asked, 'J.J. or Lee?' and Erin said that Groucho had asked the same thing. Andy Marx and Ahmet Ertegun were there too. Ahmet Ertegun was the token gentile for the evening. Mr Schubert was officiating, and after each prayer, Groucho said, 'Is this when we drink the wine?' Then there's another prayer, and Groucho says again, 'When do we drink the wine?'

Then, Mr Schubert asked, 'Can anyone play the piano? We need someone to play the hymns.' And Groucho said, 'Arthur and Andy, get to the piano!' I looked at the music, and I said to Andy, 'I can't read this. Let's play Joplin.' Well, Groucho's having the best time, and this poor man is still trying to officiate. He reads a prayer. Meanwhile, we're playing Scott Joplin, and Groucho's saying, 'When do we drink the wine?'

Mr Schubert says, '*Now* we drink the wine.'

And Groucho says, 'Do we *have* to drink the wine?'

Mr Schubert says, 'We have one more prayer.' And Groucho says, 'No, we don't. I'm gonna sing.' And with that, he goes to the piano.

It was the most irreverent religious service I have ever been to in my life.

*   *   *   *   *

A devout old Jew was grieved by the waywardness of his son, who lived in Monte Carlo and had become a gambler. To make sure the young man still observed the Jewish customs his father sent him a telegram, 'Yom Kippur starts on Sunday.'

'Put £25 on him,' came the reply.

*   *   *   *   *

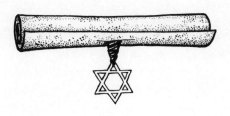

Central to many Jewish jokes and stories is the rabbi. Traditionally he held a far wider brief in his community than does his modern counterpart, who is largely a pastor, fulfilling much the same role as a Christian priest. In the villages and town of the Pale of Settlement in Russia and Poland, before its abolition after the Russian Revolution, he was everything. He was the embodiment of the law, and differences were settled in rabbinical courts. People would go to him for help on marriage matters — even for sex counselling. The rabbi in those days was judge, father confessor, friend and teacher. He was all those things and probably a very good gin rummy player into the bargain.

Rabbis still survive in that mould in orthodox communities, but the majority have shed their wider social influence. Reform rabbis of the more liberal persuasion, that has grown up in America in particular, have gone even further in shedding their traditional role. There is the joke about a reform rabbi who went so far he became a Nazi! Another tells of the reform rabbi whose synagogue was so reformed he used to close it on Jewish holidays.

In all communities (even in Chelm) the rabbi is still a figure of wisdom and learning and many have developed a well-earned reputation for delivering finely judged bons mots. *Rabbi Stephen Wise, one of the pioneers of liberal Judaism in America this century, is a case in point. After*

listening to a very long sermon in a very orthodox synagogue,
he was asked for his opinion of what the rabbi had said. 'He
has the mercy of God,' replied Dr Wise. 'He endureth for
ever.'
    On another occasion he was introduced to a politician
who had a very dubious record. 'I don't need an
introduction,' the politician told their host, 'Dr Wise has
denounced me in his sermons often enough.'
    'Often, yes,' said Dr Wise, 'but not enough.'

The Austrian Emperor Franz Josef, who took a liberal
attitude to the Jews in his domains, was in the habit of visiting
a synagogue in Cracow where his portrait was on display. Just
before one visit, however, the portrait went missing and with
the Emperor on the point of arriving there was no time to find
a substitute.

When he noticed that his picture was no longer hanging in
the synagogue, the Emperor asked the Rabbi of Cracow,
Simon Soifer, for an explanation.

'Your Majesty,' he replied, 'Jews pray daily, wearing
tefillin — two thin leather straps with small square black
leather boxes containing four passages from Exodus and
Deuteronomy in Hebrew. That is a symbol of their belief.
However, they are forbidden to wear *tefillin* on the Sabbath,
because no smaller symbol may be substituted for it on this
holy day. The same is true of Your Majesty's portrait. When
you are not with us, we have the picture to remind us of you;
but when you honour us with a visit in person, we have no
need of the picture.'

And through his inspired reasoning, this visit of Franz Josef
passed as amicably as every other one had done.

A rabbi, about to begin the late afternoon service, found that
he was a man short to complete the *minyan*, the quorum
required for a religious service. Looking out of the window for
another man he saw a known atheist standing across the
street.

'Call him in,' the rabbi told the sexton.

'Him! But he doesn't believe a word of what we say,'
complained the sexton.'

'Never mind,' the rabbi reassured him. 'We don't need
more than a nought to make the number up to ten.'

*   *   *   *   *

A Jew attending a synagogue in a strange town one Sabbath
was struck by the rabbi's insistence that life in the other world
had an importance far beyond life on earth. In particular he
was impressed by the rabbi's conviction that those who are
rich in this life will be poor in the next and vice versa.

The following day he went to the rabbi and asked him to
confirm what he had said. 'Is it true what you said yesterday,
rabbi, that he who is poor in this world will be wealthy in the
world to come?'

'Absolutely,' said the rabbi. 'There's no doubt about it.'

'In that case, rabbi, will you lend me a thousand marks,'
the Jew asked, 'and I promise to pay it back in the next
world?'

To his surprise the rabbi agreed and handed him the
money asking, 'What are you going to do with it, may I ask?'

'I hope to go into business.'

'Will you be successful and make money?'

'I hope so, if I'm lucky.'

'In that case I cannot give you the thousand marks,' said
the rabbi, taking it back as readily as he had given it.

'Why did you do that, rabbi?' asked the Jew in some
confusion.

'Well, if you are going to become rich in this world,'

55

explained the rabbi, 'you'll be poor in the next one and you won't be able to give me back my money, will you?'

*   *   *   *   *

Two young rabbis, rivals for a pulpit in a European city, were asked for interview. They arrived the night before and stayed in adjoining rooms of a local hotel.

One of the candidates, Berman, had written out a sermon to deliver the next day and he practised it remorselessly throughout the night, reading it out loud time after time.

The second candidate, however, whose name was Abelson, had forgotten to prepare anything and he went to bed early.

When the morning came, the elders of the community called the applicants in alphabetical order.

Abelson was summoned and he proceeded to deliver the sermon he had heard repeated so many times the night before in the next room.

Now poor Berman heard this but when his turn finally came he had no choice except to repeat the same talk which he had prepared the previous night.

The interview panel hurriedly met in closed session and after some discussion a decision was reached. If a man could hear a sermon only once and then repeat it word for word he must have a remarkable memory, they said.

And so Berman was elected rabbi.

*   *   *   *   *

As one of his representatives at the Vatican when Paul VI became Pope, President Kennedy sent the Orthodox rabbi Dr Louis Finkelstein.

On his way to Rome he stopped over in Paris for a few days where leading French rabbis entertained him by dining him at some of the city's foremost kosher restaurants.

'I can't understand all this fuss people make about French cooking,' Finkelstein confided to one of his friends. 'We eat just the same things at home.'

*   *   *   *   *

One day Mr Cohen arrived at *shull* (synagogue) with a dog. Waiting at the gates was the rabbi, who stopped Cohen as he was about to enter.

'Mr Cohen,' he said, 'where are you going with that dog?'

'To *shull*,' replied Cohen. 'It's nearly time for Friday night prayers.'

'I'm sorry, Mr Cohen, but you can't take a dog in there, it's not allowed.'

Cohen protested. 'But rabbi, this isn't an ordinary dog, it's a Jewish dog! It can pray, it can do everything. . . . ' Thereupon Cohen placed a little *cupple* (headcovering) on the dog and it began to *doven* (pray). It was brilliant, so good, in fact, that the rabbi asked it to take the evening service.

The dog prayed and read from the Law with such spirit and with such clarity that the assembled congregation were speechless. It took *mincha* and *ma'ariv* (the afternoon and evening services) up on its two little paws, swayed and wailed, and read Hebrew word-perfect. At the end of the service the dog removed its *tallis* (prayer shawl) and put it in the bag, shaking hands with many fellow worshippers who had crowded around to wish him *Shecoyach* (Well done!)

The rabbi went over to Mr Cohen, who was naturally gleaming with pride.

'Mr Cohen, what a magnificent dog you have there! Superb! Maybe he should consider becoming a rabbi?'

'You tell him,' said Cohen. 'He wants to become a doctor!'

*   *   *   *   *

Recalling his childhood in New York as one of eight offspring of an impoverished rabbi, the American comedian Zero Mostel once commented, 'My father brought home some poor man for almost every meal. I don't know where he found them . . . in the synagogue, on the streets, who knows? Most of them were dirty, and once I asked him why all the poor men he brought home were so dirty. Know what he said? "The clean ones, the rich get."'

*   *   *   *   *

A young rabbi, recently installed among his congregation, noticed that one elderly man occupied the same seat every Saturday afternoon and always fell asleep at the same point in the service — just as the rabbi started his sermon.

At the end of each service he was always one of the most enthusiastic in his praise of what the rabbi had said, and at first the young man refrained from passing any comments of his own.

One Saturday, however, he couldn't contain himself any longer and after the old man had again thanked him fulsomely for his sermon, the rabbi replied, 'I hope you don't mind my mentioning this, but I've noticed that you always sleep through my sermons. So how come you always thank me for what I've said?'

'Look at it this way,' said the old man, smiling. 'If I didn't trust you, how could I sleep?'

*   *   *   *   *

A young rabbi was keen to show his teaching prowess during a talk to a Sunday school class. 'Now then,' he said, 'can anyone tell me why we always refer to God as "King" in our prayers?'

He looked out for a reply but the class was silent. 'I'll tell

58

you,' said the rabbi, 'it is because a King is the highest in human life.'

'But surely, rabbi,' said one of the children, 'Ace is higher than King?'

*   *   *   *   *

The rabbi announced that the Great Flood would be the subject of his next sermon. A young wealthy Jew came up to him later, full of sorrow. 'I'm very sorry, rabbi, but I will not be able to come to your service next week because I have a business meeting,' he said, 'but here's £50 for the victims.'

*   *   *   *   *

Two Jews were arguing about a burial place in a graveyard. They both wanted the grave to be theirs when they died, and they couldn't agree who had priority.

Finally they went to the local rabbi to ask for his view.

'May I suggest,' said the rabbi, 'that the person who wants to die first should get the grave!'

*   *   *   *   *

An elderly rabbi became very ill and a doctor came to see him. The doctor examined the old man and asked him how old he was. 'Ninety-four,' replied the rabbi.

'Well, I'm afraid I can't make you any younger,' said the doctor.

'I don't want to get younger,' snapped the rabbi. 'I want to get older!'

*   *   *   *   *

Rabbi Shapiro of Slonim asked his son-in-law, another rabbi, to become his associate. After some months the young rabbi went to his father-in-law and asked: 'We both teach, we both preach and we both receive the same salary — how can people tell who is the real Rabbi of Slonim?'

The senior rabbi paused and then said, 'The one who is most criticized, he is the real rabbi!'

* * * * *

A very elderly rabbi was close to death when a friend asked how old he was.

'I can't say,' said the rabbi quickly. 'When you're facing bankruptcy, you don't reveal your assets!'

* * * * *

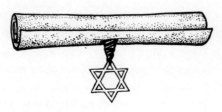

One of the strengths of Judaism is the intimacy the Jew feels with God, whom he looks on as a personal friend. God is someone with whom a Jew can converse man to man, as illustrated by one of my favourite stories of the Jew standing in the synagogue wearing his prayer shawl and little black cap with his eyes raised to heaven as he prayed, 'Oh God . . . God, I'm in such trouble. My business is going down the drain. I owe fifty thousand pounds. The income tax is demanding payment. The bank is going to foreclose. My wife has walked out on me. Am I in trouble . . .' Then he stopped, hearing a man a couple of seats along in the same pew saying, 'Oh God, I'm in such trouble. My son has run off with a non-Jewish girl. My daughter is a lesbian . . .' at which the first Jew said, 'Excuse me, here's ten pounds. Now go away. Would you let him concentrate on me, please?'

God may keep a watchful eye, sometimes critical, eye on the Jews, but he is always there and nothing — but nothing — escapes his notice.

In a synagogue a very pious-looking man with a long beard was praying. With his eyes lifted to heaven he said, 'Oh, God, have I got troubles . . . have I got troubles. My only son has changed his religion.'

There was a clap of thunder and a deep voice from above said, '*Your* only son has changed his religion!'

61

I've Taken a Page in the Bible

Early one morning on *Yom Kippur* (the Day of Atonement, when eating, drinking and other pleasures are forbidden) a young rabbi took a short cut to the temple across a golf course. On his way he found a golf club and ball lying in the grass. Looking around quickly to check if anyone was watching, he picked up the club and had a mighty swing at the ball. The ball soared away into the distance, and by amazing fortune went straight into the hole.

Up in heaven the angel and prophets were furious that the sporting rabbi had violated the holy day and asked God that he be punished.

'He has already received his punishment,' said the Lord. 'Who can he tell?'

*   *   *   *   *

A little Jew went into a snack bar and asked the price of a roast beef sandwich. When he heard what it was, he asked how much a cheese sandwich cost. Again he was told, and again he asked how much another was — a ham sandwich this time. Before the assistant had a chance to reply, a terrifying clap of thunder burst right above the snack bar.

'All right, all right,' said the Jew, falling on his knees and looking up to heaven. 'I was only asking.'

*   *   *   *   *

Three top leaders, Kruschev from Russia, De Gaulle of France and President Nasser of Egypt, went to Heaven for an audience to discover the future.

'Please tell me, Lord,' asked De Gaulle, 'how long it will be before France is once more the world's leading nation?'

'Another hundred years,' replied God.

'What!' said De Gaulle, 'not in my lifetime?'

Next it was Krushchev's turn. 'Please could you tell me,' he said, 'how long before the Soviet Union dominates the whole world?'

'It will take another two hundred years,' said God.

'What!' cried Kruschev, 'not in my lifetime?'

Finally it was Nasser's turn to ask a question. 'Please, Almighty, ' he began, 'when will I be able to destroy Israel?'

'NOT IN MY LIFETIME!' thundered the Almighty.

*   *   *   *   *

An elderly Jew explained to his grandson why the Ten Commandments were written on two tablets of stone instead of one.

At first God had approached the French to see if they wanted the Commandments. 'Never,' said the French, 'we cannot accept "Thou shalt not commit adultery" — it is part of our culture!'

So the God went to Scotland to see if they would like the Commandments there. 'How can we love our neighbours,' asked the Scots, 'when we live next to the English?' And the Scots, too, turned them down.

In the end God went to the Jews and asked if *they* wanted the Commandments.

'How much?' said the Jews.

'They're free,' said God.

'We'll take two,' said the Jews.

*   *   *   *   *

A grandfather and his little grandson were praying side by side in the synagogue.

The little boy was muttering away in a barely audible voice and his grandfather clipped him round the ear and told him, 'I can't hear a word you're saying.'

'I'm not talking to you,' said his grandson indignantly.

In communities during the middle ages it was traditional to 'ask' the recently deceased to plead with God for the well-being of the the town.

Once an eight-year-old boy died and the leader of the community was about to ask the child's spirit to intervene on the town's behalf when a Jew, who disliked the leader, stopped him.

'Surely,' said the Jew, 'you can't trust a child with such an important task as this — why not go yourself?'

* * * * *

Some of the funniest Jewish stories I have ever heard have been told to me by goyim, *non-Jews, and the relationship between the Jews and those of other religions, particularly Christians, has been the breeding ground of a rich store of Jewish humour.*

I remember with great affection an evening in Dublin thirty years ago when, after a one-man show I was doing, a party of broken-nosed, cauliflower-eared, beer-swilling rugby players came back-stage and introduced themselves as theological students from a Roman Catholic seminary. We went back to the Gresham Hotel where I was staying and there we had a session lasting till four in the morning, sinking beer and telling stories. I found that I couldn't get a word in for most of the evening, but I was quite content to listen to them rattling off some of the best stories in this book — as well as a good many that didn't show their own following in a very favourable light!

Perhaps the relationship between Jews and Gentiles is most neatly summed up in Leo Rosten's response to the rhyme:

How odd
Of God
To choose
The Jews

to which the American writer and compiler of The Joys of Yiddish *and* Hooray for Yiddish!, *two of the most entertaining and instructive glossaries of the language, was inspired to write:*

Not odd
Of God
Goyim
Annoy 'im

A Jew and a Catholic who were good friends each had a son to embark on a career. The Jew's boy was to become a solicitor, while the Catholic's had entered a seminary to prepare for the priesthood.

The Jew was curious about his son's friend. 'What happens to him when he becomes a priest?' he asked his friend.

'After a while he can become a bishop,' replied the Catholic.

'And then?'

'If he is good, he could make it to archbishop, and even cardinal.'

'So is that the top?' asked the Jew.

'Well, no,' replied the Catholic with a smile. 'If he is very lucky he could become Pope!'

'Is that all?' asked the Jew.

His friend was taken aback. 'What do you mean,' he asked sarcastically. 'Did you expect him to become the Lord?'

'Why not?' replied the Jew. 'You think one of our boys did!'

*   *   *   *   *

The Jewish philosopher Moses Mendelsohn was asked to a banquet by the Kaiser, at which he sat next to a Catholic bishop.

The meat dishes arrived at the table and Mendelsohn asked for a vegetable dish instead, as the meat was non-kosher.

'Really, Dr Mendelsohn,' the bishop remarked, 'when will you abandon your old-fashioned superstitions and eat like the rest of us?'

'At your marriage feast,' replied Mendelsohn.

*   *   *   *   *

A rabbi and a Catholic priest were travelling opposite each other on a train and the priest asked the rabbi after a while, 'Tell me, rabbi, as a man of the cloth in your faith you're not supposed to eat pork, are you?'

'That is correct.'

'Tell me then, man to man, have you ever tried it?'

'When I was a young man,' the rabbi answered, 'I must confess that I did try it. Tell me, father, as a man of the cloth in your faith, you're not supposed to have sexual relations with women, are you?'

'No, that's right.'

'Would you tell me, man to man, have you ever tried that?'

'To be honest with you,' said the Catholic leader, 'when I was a young man I did try it.'

'Hm...', reflected the rabbi. 'Better than pork, isn't it?'

*   *   *   *   *

One day a vicar passed on and headed for the Gates of Paradise. He was met by an angel, who asked for his name. On hearing it, the angel said: 'Mr Brown, for all your good deeds on earth, and the visits to your community, the Heavenly Tribunal has awarded you this BMX bicycle. It's yours to use in heaven for ever!'

Brown was very pleased and rode off on his bike to explore heaven. Then suddenly he saw Father O'Malley in a brand new Mini Metro. As fast as he could, he raced back to the gates and spoke to the angel.

'Why has Father O'Malley got a Mini Metro when I've only got a bike?' he asked.

'Well,' said the angel, 'while on earth you visited your flock in a car, while Father O'Malley had no car and had to walk. Thus, up here, you get a bicycle and Father O'Malley gets a Mini Metro.'

Contented enough with the justice of this statement, the vicar continued on his journey, riding around, whistling and singing away... until he caught sight of Rabbi Green riding around in a brand-new white Rolls Royce convertible. This was too much! He rushed back to the angel. 'I quite understand about Father O'Malley,' he said, 'because he had to walk around the place, but I happen to remember Rabbi Green on earth! He used to have a beautiful Porsche 924!!'

'Shhhhh...' said the angel. 'He's a friend of the boss!'

*   *   *   *   *

Father Murphy was chatting to Rabbi Chomsky one day, when the subject turned to ways of popularizing their faiths. 'The trouble with you Jews,' said Father Murphy, 'is that you are too set in your ways. You never try anything new, like advertising on television to get your message across. Truly, the modern world is leaving you behind.'

'Father Murphy,' replied Rabbi Chomsky, 'you obviously know nothing of our Jewish history. After all, Samson had this advertising thing taped over three thousand years ago — he took two columns and brought down the house!'

*   *   *   *   *

A rabbi and a priest were discussing their respective faiths while walking through a garden filled with flowers.

'You see these flowers,' said the priest. 'They are the different races that make up the Christian Church. Show me where your race is.'

The rabbi led him to the garden fence where brambles were growing on the other side and said, 'This is our race.'

'Are you being serious?' asked the priest, suspecting that his analogy was being mocked.

'Of course I am,' replied the rabbi. 'Anyone can do what he wants with your flowers, but just try touching our brambles and they'll feel the difference.'

68

Leah took her grandmother to the movies as a treat, and it happened to be a 'Roman' epic. When it came to the amphitheatre scene in which people were being thrown to the lions and wild beasts, Leah's grandmother became very upset. 'Sh, grandma. They're not real Christians; it's only a film.'

Grandmother hadn't realized they were Christians and was pacified. Only for a moment, however, before she again started to make agitated noises.

'What's the matter now?' asked her exasperated grand-daughter.

'That poor little lion, there, at the side,' said grandma, 'he's not getting anything to eat!'

*   *   *   *   *

A popular story from a quarter of a century ago was centred on the US-USSR non aggression pact that was due to be signed by Kruschev and Kennedy. However, before the Russian leader agreed to put his name to the document he insisted that Kennedy announce publicly that Adam and Eve were Communists.

Anxious to offend neither Jewish nor Christian communities and uncertain what he should do, Kennedy approached Israel's venerable premier, David Ben-Gurion, an acknowledged authority on the Bible.

'Certainly you can say they were Communists,' he reassured the American president. 'After all, they didn't have a stitch of clothing between them; they had nothing to live on but apples; and still they believed they were in Paradise.'

*   *   *   *   *

A synagogue and a Catholic church stood side by side in New York. The rabbi and the priest were very good friends and often shared ideas with each other on ecumenical matters. By coincidence they both bought new cars at the same time and the morning after collecting his, the rabbi was very touched to see the Catholic father blessing it with holy water. So to reciprocate, he sawed a couple of inches off the exhaust pipe of the priest's car.

*　　*　　*　　*　　*

A Jew who had lived in Germany for many years finally decided to become a convert and embrace Christianity as his new religion.

When he was standing waiting to be baptized, the pastor asked him what name he would like to take as a Christian.

'Martin Luther,' he replied.

The pastor was shocked. 'Martin Luther, the founder of German Protestantism? That is a very famous name. Tell me, why do you choose that name?'

'It's like this, father,' answered the man, 'My name is Manny Leibowitz, and I thought, why go to all the trouble of changing the initials on my shirts!'

*　　*　　*　　*　　*

A family were going round an art gallery when they came across a classic picture of the Holy Family, the infant Christ in the manger with Joseph and Mary looking down at him.

'Just like the bleeding Jews,' said the father. 'Haven't got a room for the night and still get the bloody family portrait painted by Rubens.'

*　　*　　*　　*　　*

'I'd like to speak to Mr Horowitz, please,' said a voice down the line to a switch-board operator.

'I'm sorry, sir, Mr Horowitz isn't in the office, this is Yom Kippur,' she explained. 'Can I take a message for him?'

Well, Miss Kippur, when do you expect him back?'

While Arthur Miller was engaged to Marilyn Monroe, he took her home to meet his very Jewish mother on a Friday night when she had prepared the Sabbath dinner. The old lady welcomed them, and after sitting them at the table gave them the first course, saying, 'Here you are — chicken soup with *motza* balls for you, darling.'

The next week she served the same soup and the same dumplings made from *motza* flour — and the week after that. As they were driving away after the third visit, Marilyn Monroe asked Miller, 'Do you people ever eat any other part of the *motza*?'

*　　*　　*　　*　　*

Since the majority of Ireland's small Jewish population belongs to the orthodox faith, the construction of a reform synagogue in Dublin caused some confusion, especially among the ninety-five per cent of the population that were Roman Catholics. One Dublin taxi driver was asked by his passenger what the new building was and replied uncertainly, 'That?... Oh, it's the new Protestant synagogue.'

*　　*　　*　　*　　*

During New York's 'Bloomsbury period' in the 1920s and '30s, the Algonquin Hotel became a famous meeting point for the leading lights in the city's literary set, particular writers connected with the *New Yorker* like Dorothy Parker, Robert Benchley and the editor Franklin Pierce Adams. The Algonquin's dining-room had a round table at which this select band got into the habit of lunching, and the fame of the Algonquin Round Table — as the group came to be known — spread far beyond Manhattan.

One of the frequent members of the group was the playwright George S. Kaufman, who was often the target of

71

critic Alexander Woollcott's playful reference to his Jewish ancestry. On one occasion Woollcott pushed Kaufman a little too far and in feigned disgust he got to his feet and announced, 'I have had enough of Mr Woollcott's slurs on my race. I am leaving this table and this dining-room and this hotel.'

Then looking round the table, he fixed his eyes on Dorothy Parker — whose mother was Scots and father Jewish — and concluded, 'And I trust that Mrs Parker will walk out with me — half-way!'

*   *   *   *   *

A similar story tells that after a man at another dinner had boasted excessively about the long and pristine line of his Christian forebears, tracing his ancestry right back to the eleventh century, Kaufman rose to leave the table, but not before remarking that one of his own ancestors had taken part in a crusade — Sir Roderick Kaufman. His adversary looked completely non-plussed before Kaufman added, 'As a spy, of course.'

*   *   *   *   *

'Ah, ha!' said the plastic surgeon, removing the bandages from the Jewish actor whose nose he had been straightening. 'A thing of beauty and a goy for ever.'

*   *   *   *   *

Caption to cartoon depicting the meeting between the Pope and the President of Israel in 1964: 'The Pope is the one with the *yarmulkah* (skullcap).'

*   *   *   *   *

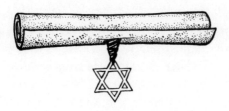

Sholom Aleichem is probably the most universally famous Yiddish writer. Solomon Rabinovitch (his real name) took the daily greeting of the Jews, which means 'Peace be with you', and used it as his pen name. His stories breathe the life, vitality, contradictions and frustrations felt by so many Jews, and this story, taken from Maurice Samuel's collection The World of Sholom Aleichem, *is a fine example of his retelling of a traditional Jewish story.*

Years ago, when I was still a young man, I was living in a little town which was blessed with a total of nine Jewish families. How did I make a living? I kept a hotel. I bought and sold wheat. I picked up odd lots of any kind of merchandise. Between one thing and another, I just about managed. One fine day, right in the midst of the wheat season, my wife takes it into her mind to be delivered of a child — a boy! *Mazel tov!* But a boy means a circumcision ceremony on the eighth day, doesn't he? And a circumcision ceremony means a quorum of ten Jews, doesn't it? And there are only nine adult Jews in town, including myself. What's to be done? Where am I to get a tenth Jew in that Godforsaken townlet?

On the eighth day after my son's birth I went down to the railroad station, hoping against hope that a Jewish traveller

73

would get off the train and I could invite him to the house for the ceremony. It was a Friday afternoon. Sure enough, when our one daily train drew in, there steps off a respectable-looking Jew, carrying his valise. He rushes over to the lunch-counter and looks hungrily at the collection of cakes, sandwiches, beer-bottles — you know the kind of stuff they keep on those counters: half of it ham, all of it uneatable. I go up to him: 'Mr Jew, how would you like to earn yourself a portion in paradise, and at the same time eat a good solid meal, a plate of golden-yellow soup, a steaming goulash that melts in your mouth, and white Sabbath bread fresh out of the oven?' The man looks at me as if I'd taken leave of my senses. 'Listen, man,' I say to him, 'it's a question of life and death, or pretty near to it: a question of inducting a little Jew into the congregation of Israel' — and I explain the whole business to him.

'But I've got to catch that train!' he says. 'I've got to be in Yehupetz before nightfall.' 'Yehupetz, shmehupetz,' I answer him. 'Do you or don't you want to earn yourself a portion in paradise? Do you or don't you want to eat a good solid meal, Jewish cooking, a goulash that melts in your mouth, golden-yellow soup, white Sabbath bread fresh out of the oven?' And without waiting for his answer, I grab his valise and run off with it. What could the poor man do? He followed!

Well, we had our tenth man, and the circumcision ceremony was performed according to the law and tradition. And my traveller, my life-saver, got a meal that evening that would have made a king's mouth water. My woman was already on her feet, and cooking, and without boasting, I can say that my woman's cooking hasn't its equal in Poltava or even in the rest of Russia.

That was a Friday evening, you understand. No question of my guest moving for twenty-four hours. And on the next day, on the Sabbath, I say to him: 'You've saved a Jewish soul, do you understand? I can't speak of a reward — there's no reward big enough. But today you're going to eat a piece of roast chicken that you'll remember the rest of your life. An hors d'oeuvre of chopped onion and goose-fat, with a couple of glasses of brandy, and a roast chicken — my wife's work, that'll leave you homesick for this town. You understand?' Sure he understood. But when Sunday morning came, and he made ready to resume his journey, I say to him: 'Are you out of your mind? Do you think I'm going to let you go just like that? A man who saved a Jewish soul, so to speak, a man sent to me from heaven? No, sir. You're going to stay here and taste my wife's borscht, because unless you come this way again you'll never taste borscht like that as long as you live.' And let me tell you, *Rabbiner*, that was borscht out of borscht-land: with a couple of crisp potato pancakes, and a glass or two of red wine — what's the use of talking! My man grumbled, but smacked his lips.

And then, on Monday morning, he *must* be leaving of course. 'Not on your life!' I tell him. 'This is the third day after the circumcision. Don't you know that on the third day after the circumcision it's usual to hold a special feast? And do you think after all this I'll let you walk off like a stranger? Wait! You're going to eat dairy *varnishkes* this evening that'll open your eyes! I wouldn't let you miss those *varnishkes* for anything in the world.' My man begins to yell: 'Murder! Is there no pity in your bosom? I've business to attend to.' 'Business-shmizzness,' I tell him. 'A plateful of my wife's dairy *varnishkes*, with a couple of bottles of beer, is the best business in the world.' And sure enough, I made him stay. I made him stay four days with me, and only on the fifth day did I let him pack his valise. And just as he was about to leave, I handed him a bill.

He looked at me, sort of dazed. 'What's this?' 'The bill,' I said; 'thirty-seven roubles and fifteen kopecks. It's itemized.' 'The bill,' he repeated in a whisper, then let out a yell. 'The bill? Isn't it enough that you killed four days for me, held me by the throat, after I'd done you the service of attending the circumcision ceremony of your new-born son. What is this? A joke? Or a hold-up?' 'It isn't a joke, mister,' I tell him, 'and it isn't a hold-up. It's just a simple reckoning. I'm not charging you for the first afternoon — that was your good deed for the day. But there was no good deed involved in your staying here, eating your head off, drinking my best cognac and wine and beer, for four days.' 'Then why did you plead with me to stay?' 'Salesmanship,' I answered.

Well, Rabbi, the poor man was a sight! He couldn't get it into his head that bed and board cost money. At last I said to him: 'Listen. Do we have to quarrel? There's a *Rabbiner* in the next townlet, an honourable gentleman, a scholar and a sage. Suppose we put it up to him? I pledge myself in advance to accept his decision.'

Done! We get into the train, proceed to the next townlet, and go to the Rabbi — the *Rabbiner*, that is. My 'guest' lets loose, dishes up the story from beginning to end, omitting not a detail. The *Rabbiner* listens, patiently, just as you did, to the very end, then turns to me and asks: 'Well, what have you to say?' 'Me?' I answer. 'I've nothing at all to say. This gentleman has told you nothing but the truth.' With that the *Rabbiner* turns back to my guest, asks him again how long he had stayed with me, what he had eaten, what he drank, whether he was satisfied with the cooking, did he enjoy the cognac — and when the second recital is over, the *Rabbiner* shrugs his shoulders, looks at me knowingly, and says to my guest: 'Sorry! You'll have to pay!'

The man turned green, yellow, and purple. But he pulled out a fifty-rouble note and flung it in my face. 'Here,' he said. 'Give me the change.' 'Change?' I said. 'What are you talking about? Who wants your money? Take back your fifty-rouble note, man. What do you take me for? Isn't it enough that you saved a Jewish soul, helped me to induct my son into the congregation of Israel, gave me the pleasure of your company for four days? Do you expect me to charge you for it? Is this Sodom and Gomorrah?'

Well, the man was absolutely flabbergasted. 'For God's sake!' he gasped. 'What is this? What did you want the whole comedy for? Why did you drag me here?'

'Just like that,' I answered. 'I wanted to show you what a clever Rabbi we've got.'

A more up-to-date impression of Judaism that reflects the contrasts and conflicts of the orthodox and reform faiths is given by the Canadian writer Mordecai Richler. This extract is taken from his novel The Apprenticeship of Duddy Kravitz *which was first published in 1959.*

The Cohen boy's *bar mitzvah* was a big affair in a modern synagogue. The synagogue in fact was so modern that it was not called a synagogue any more. It was called a Temple. Duddy had never seen anything like it in his life. There was a choir and an organ and a parking lot next door. The men not only did not wear hats but they sat together with the women. All these things were forbidden by traditional Jewish law, but those who attended the Temple were so-called reform Jews and they had modernized the law to suit life in America. The Temple prayer services were conducted in English by Rabbi Harvey Goldstone, M.A., and Cantor 'Sonny' Brown. Aside from his weekly sermon, the marriage clinic, the Sunday school, and so on, the Rabbi, a most energetic man, was very active in the community at large. He was a fervent supporter of Jewish and Gentile Brotherhood, and a man who unfailingly offered his time to radio stations as a spokesman for the Jewish point of view on subjects that ranged from 'Does Israel Mean Divided Loyalties?' to 'The Jewish Attitude to Household Pets'. He also wrote articles for

78

magazines and a weekly column of religious comfort for the *Tely*. There was a big demand for Rabbi Goldstone as a public speaker and he always made sure to send copies of his speeches to all the newspapers and radio stations.

Mr Cohen, who was on the Temple executive, was one of the Rabbi's most enthusiastic supporters, but there were some who did not approve. He was, as one magazine writer had put it, a controversial figure.

'The few times I stepped inside there,' Dingleman once said. 'I felt like a Jesuit in a whorehouse.'

But Mr Cohen, Farber, and other leaders of the community all took seats at the temple for the High Holidays on, as Mr Cohen said, the forty-yard line. The Rabbi was extremely popular with the young-marrieds and that, their parents felt, was important. Otherwise, some said with justice, the children would never learn about their Jewish heritage.

Another dissenter was Uncle Benjy. 'There used to be,' he said, 'some dignity in being against the synagogue. With a severe orthodox rabbi there were things to quarrel about. There was some pleasure. But this cream-puff of a synagogue, this religious drugstore, you might as well spend your life being against the *Reader's Digest*. They've taken all the mystery out of religion.'

At the *bar mitzvah* Mr Cohen had trouble with his father. The old rag peddler was, he feared, stumbling on the edge of senility. He still clung to his cold-water flat on St Dominique Street and was a fierce follower of a Chassidic rabbi there. He had never been to the Temple before. Naturally he would not drive on the Sabbath and so that morning he had got up at six and walked more than five miles to make sure to be on time for the first prayers. As Mr Friar stood by with his camera to get the three generations together Mr Cohen and his son came down the outside steps to greet the old man. The old man stumbled. 'Where's the synagogue?' he asked.

'This is it, Paw. This is the Temple.'

The old man looked up at the oak doors and the magnificent stained glass windows. 'It's a church,' he said, retreating.

'It's the Temple, Paw. This is where Bernie is going to be *bar mitzvah.*'

'Would the old chap lead him up the steps by the hand?' Mr Friar asked.

'Shettup,' Duddy said.

The old man retreated down another step.

'This is the *shul*, Paw. Come on.'

'It's a church.'

Mr Cohen laughed nervously. 'Paw, for Christ's sake!' And he led the old man forcefully up the steps. 'Stop sniffing. This isn't a funeral.'

Inside, the services began. 'Turn to page forty-one in your prayer books, please,' Rabbi Goldstone said. 'Blessed is the Lord, Our Father...'

The elder Cohen began to sniffle again.

'Isn't he sweet,' somebody said.

'Bernie's the only grandchild.'

Following the *bar mitzvah* ceremony, Rabbi Goldstone began his sermon. 'This,' he said, 'is National Sports Week.' He spoke on Jewish Athletes — From Bar Kochva to Hank Greenberg. Afterwards he had some announcements to make. He reminded the congregation that if they took a look at the racehorse chart displayed in the hall they would see that 'Jewish History' was trailing 'Dramatics Night' by five lengths. He hoped that more people would attend the next lecture. The concealed organ began to play and the Rabbi, his voice quivering, read off an anniversary list of members of the congregation who over the years had departed for the great beyond. He began to read the Mourner's Prayer as Mr Friar, his camera held to his eye, tip-toed nearer for a medium close shot.

The elder Cohen had begun to weep again when the first chord had been struck on the organ and Mr Cohen had had to take him outside. 'You lied to me,' he said to his son. 'It is a church.'

* * * * *

'Never mind what Nasser will say! You should have heard what my Aunt Rosie said!'
Barbra Streisand, after being seen kissing Omar Sharif in the film Funny Girl

* * * * *

A rabbi whom they don't want to drive out of town isn't a rabbi, and a rabbi whom they actually drive out isn't a man.
Israel Lipkin

* * * * *

If thy tongue offend thee tear it out.
If thine eye offend thee pluck it out.
If thy hand offend thee cut it off.
If thy brain offend thee, turn Catholic.
Heinrich Heine

* * * * *

Yes, I am a Jew, and when the ancestors of the right honourable gentleman were brutal savages in an unknown island, mine were priests in the Temple of Solomon.
Benjamin Disraeli, to the Irish MP Daniel O'Connell

* * * * *

Naturally God will forgive me. That's his business.
Heinrich Heine's last words

Business is Business

or borrow your way out of debt

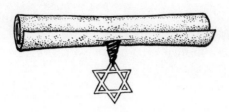

For many people business and Jews are one and the same, and this stems from a reputation built up through the hundreds of years when Jews were forbidden from following trades, which left them with nothing to do but trade with each other.

By nature, of course, the Jew is a farmer, as is being proved in Israel; though the idea of a Jewish farmer in England seems unlikely. Restricted to dealing within their own communities Jews developed a canny instinct for the ways of business, helped no doubt by their Middle Eastern legacy and the tradition of the great trading centres linked by caravan routes and merchant ships.

The pragmatism that colours much of the psychology of the Jew is shown up especially in the humour of the business world, as this comment from James Seligman suggests:

'To sell something you have, to someone who wants it — that is not business. But to sell something you don't have to someone who doesn't want it — that is business.'

'Father,' whispered his son who was learning the business. 'There is a customer in the shop who wants to know if one of those all-wool unshrinkable shirts will shrink.'

'Does it fit him?'

'No, it's too large.'

'Well, then, it'll shrink.'

*   *   *   *   *

An old Jew was crossing a golf course with no idea he was running the risk of being hit, when a golf-ball smacked into the back of his neck.

'I'm going to sue someone for this,' he screamed in rage. 'I'm not going to settle for less than ten thousand pounds!'

'Fore!' shouted a voice in the distance.

'OK — I'll take four thousand,' shouted back the Jew.

*   *   *   *   *

'Who was your last employer?' a personnel manager asked an applicant for a new job in a men's wear shop.

'Bernstein and Goldman,' said the applicant confidently.

'And how long were you with them?'

'Forty years.'

'How old are you?' asked the manager, slightly taken aback by this reply from such a young-looking man.

'Thirty-eight,' he said.

'Thirty-eight? So how did you work for forty years?'

'I did a lot of overtime.'

*   *   *   *   *

'If I loaned your father fifty dollars to be paid back at ten dollars a month, how much would he owe me at the end of five months?' a teacher asked a Jewish boy in his class.

'Fifty-five dollars,' replied the boy in a flash.

Business is Business

'You don't know how to subtract,' snapped the teacher.
'You don't know my father,' replied the boy.

*   *   *   *   *

Cohen opened a Chinese restaurant right in the middle of Whitechapel. One of his first clients was Levine — who couldn't believe his ears when one of the Chinese waiters came to his table and proceeded to go right through the menu in fluent Yiddish. The meal was superb and, as he left, Levine thanked Cohen. Indicating the waiter, he told him, 'You're very lucky, you know, where do you get these waiters?'
'Hong Kong.'
'It's amazing — they speak perfect Yiddish.'
'Shut up,' whispered Cohen. 'They think they're speaking English.'

*   *   *   *   *

Manuel Slivowitz decided to go back and visit the country of his youth — Russia. Since his emigration to Britain as a young boy, he had become a wealthy man. In fact a very wealthy man — a millionaire!
As he was journeying across country, he stopped at a small village for lunch. The news soon spread that the man in the limousine was the famous Slivowitz, and the crowds gathered.
He entered a small, run-down café and ordered scrambled eggs. When the bill arrived, he was a little surprised to see that he was being charged 100 roubles.
'Are eggs so rare in these parts?' he asked sarcastically.
'No,' replied the owner of the café sharply, 'but Slivowitzes are!'

*   *   *   *   *

I've Taken a Page in the Bible

Schwarz, the wealthy jeweller, bumped into Holmbaum, the tailor, one day in the street. Schwarz was immaculately dressed, but Holmbaum looked a mess. His overcoat was full of holes.

'I don't believe it,' said Schwarz. 'You're a tailor, and yet you walk around with your clothes in tatters. I know you're a poor man, but *oy vey*!'

'It may seem strange to you,' answered Holmbaum, 'but I work so hard to make ends meet, to keep my family, that I just don't have time to see to my own clothes.'

'Look,' said Schwarz. 'I'm a generous man. Here's five pounds so that you can get your overcoat mended.'

Holmbaum thanked him, and they went their separate ways. A few days later they met again, and Holmbaum was still wearing the same torn overcoat.

'I don't believe it,' gasped Schwarz. 'I give you five pounds, and you still haven't mended it. What's the matter with you?'

'It's like this, Schwarz,' said Holmbaum apologetically. 'I'm grateful to you for the money, believe me, but it just wasn't enough to pay for my time!'

*　　　*　　　*　　　*　　　*

Richard Burton went into a very seedy little agent's office in Charing Cross Road. There was one rickety chair in the room, and a filthy desk behind which sat a man with a cigar — a theatrical agent named Hyman Cohen.

'Hello,' said the star.

'You're Richard Burton!'

'Yes.'

'But what are you doing here?'

'Liz and myself are fed up with these big Hollywood agents. We'd like somebody who can handle our business in London — somebody who's a bit of a hustler.'

Almost on the point of apoplexy the agent cleared the

desk of all the papers and dusted off the chair, offering it to his visitor.

'We want somebody fresh,' Burton continued. 'These Hollywood lawyers and people, they don't really work for you and we wondered if you could take us on. . . . By the way, Mr Cohen, you're not Jewish are you?'

'Not necessarily,' responded Cohen.

*   *   *   *   *

Turning his attention from his world-famous department store in New York, Alfred Bloomingdale once produced a musical, which had its pre-Broadway opening in Boston. The critics were not enthusiastic and when Bloomingdale asked George S. Kaufman for his opinion, Kaufman told him, 'If I were you, I'd close the show and keep the store open nights.'

*   *   *   *   *

An American teacher spoke to her class at school, trying to get a little enthusiasm into them.

'I'll give ten dollars to the first person to tell me who the most important person in the Bible was,' she promised.

Hands shot up. 'Simon Cohen,' said the teacher.

Simon stood up. 'It's Jesus Christ, ma'am,' he said.

'Well done,' said the teacher, somewhat surprised. She continued, 'I'll give another ten dollars to the first person to tell me why Jesus was the most important person in the Bible.'

Again Simon Cohen's hand shot up first.

'Simon?'

'Because he is the Son of God,' said Simon.

'Well done,' said the teacher.

At the end of the lesson, when the class left, the teacher called Simon to her desk. 'Look, Simon,' she said, 'here's the twenty dollars you won in my class today, but I'm a little surprised that you, a Jewish boy, should have got the answer right. Why did you say Jesus?'

'Actually, ma'am,' said the boy, 'I think the answer's Moses, but business is business!'

* * * * *

A top American doctor was known for his very high fees, but he never charged the clergy for treatment. When a Catholic priest came for an examination and asked what the fee was, the doctor replied, 'Nothing.' To show his thanks the priest sent him a small silver cross. The second patient was a Protestant vicar, who, in gratitude for the free treatment, sent the doctor a bound leather bible.

The third patient was a rabbi. He sent him another rabbi!

* * * * *

The wealthy Baron Rothschild received a letter from a Jew claiming to have the secret of immortality. Naturally the Baron was interested in this, and wrote back inviting the man to visit him.

One day, sure enough, the Jew turned up at his office.

'What is the secret you talk of?' asked the Baron.

'First you must give me $500,' said the Jew.

Still eager to hear how he might live for ever, the Baron handed over the cash. 'Now tell me,' he demanded. 'What is the secret?'

'You must come and live in my town,' replied the Jew, 'for no millionaire has ever passed away there!'

* * * * *

Einstein's theory of relativity was still fairly new stuff, and a perplexed old Jew asked his son to explain it to him. The son didn't know where to begin, naturally enough, but, after a moment's reflection he said, 'Well, Papa, it's something like this; you go to the dentist, see, and you sit there in his chair and a minute seems like an hour. Now you imagine that you're sitting with a lovely girl on your knee, and a hour would seem like a minute. That's a bit like Einstein's theory.'

The old man gazed at his son. 'And from this he makes a living?'

* * * * *

A hard-nosed Jewish businessman hated liberalism and any suggestion of state welfare. When Franklin D. Roosevelt became President of the United States he was very angry. He used to buy a newspaper every day, read the front page, then throw it in the bin.

Once a friend of his asked him why he did this.

'I'm searching for an obituary,' said the Jew.

'Well, you won't find it there. The obituaries are always on page eight,' said his friend.

'Not the one I'm looking for,' snarled the Jew.

* * * * *

A customer walked into a Jewish tailor's shop in the East End in the 1960s and asked if he could make him a Beatle jacket.

'A Beatle jacket? What's a Beatle jacket?' asked the tailor.

'It's like an ordinary jacket but with no collar...' 'No collar,' repeated the tailor, writing down the details.

'Yes... there's no lining...'

'No lining.'

'No lapels...'

'No lapels.'

'No button-holes...'

'No button-holes.'

'No buttons...'

'No buttons.'

'That's it. Now, how much are you going to charge me?'
'Well,' said the tailor, 'ordinarily a jacket would be fifteen pounds, but with all these extras. . . . '

*   *   *   *   *

A man went into a New York Jewish tailor's shop and said, 'I'd like a sports coat making, please.'
'Certainly, sir,' said the tailor.
'This is a special sports coat, you understand. It's got to be made of genuine Harris tweed.'
'Sure — Harris tweed.'
'Yeah, well, how long is it going to take?'
'Well, if it's going to be genuine Harris tweed, I'll fly out on the first plane to London. That'll take a day. Then I'll get a connection to Edinburgh. Then I'll have to take the train and boat to the islands. I know the crofters very well and they'll let me select the warp and the weft. I'll also choose the sheep and supervise the weaving and dyeing. Then it'll have to be hung and dried. Then I'll have to select who is going to weave the cloth. Once that's done I'll come back to New York to get the patterns ready. Then the cloth will have to go through the bonded warehouse to clear customs before I can get to work on it. The whole job will take about two months.'
'That's no good,' said the customer, 'I've got to have it Friday.'
'You'll have it Friday,' promised the tailor.

*   *   *   *   *

Teacher: How many seasons are there in the year?
Little Jewish boy: Two — busy and slack!

*   *   *   *   *

'Cohen,' said the maths teacher to her primary school class.
   'Yes,' said the little seven-year-old boy standing up.
   'What's two per cent of a thousand pounds?'
   'I'm not interested, miss.'

       *   *   *   *   *

A Jew was once asked to define an optimist.
   'He is a Jew who buys from another Jew, sells to a Scotsman and still expects to make a profit!'

       *   *   *   *   *

'I'm very sorry to hear about your fire last Tuesday.'
   'Shush! It's next Tuesday.'

       *   *   *   *   *

The plight of the schnorrer *and the commonly impoverished state of the* schlemiel *typify the grinding poverty endured by so many Jews for so long. And this concern (some might say preoccupation) with money and ways of saving it forms the backbone to much Jewish humour, as well as a good deal of the humour directed at Jews by* goyim.

It is for this reason too that the few wealthy Jews of the past, notably the Rothschilds, were held up as figures of wonder to the Jews of the Russian Pale who were kept virtually on the breadline by state legislation.

One day a Jewish man was knocked over by a huge lorry and lay dying in the road. A doctor came rushing out of one of the nearby houses and propped up his head, loosened his collar and took his pulse.

'Are you comfortable?' he asked.

'Thank God, I made a living!'

*   *   *   *   *

An elderly Jewish man was indignant when a letter he had posted was returned to him, and he went to the post office to complain. 'Why has this letter come back to me?' he asked a clerk.

94

'Because the value of stamps you put on it were not enough for the weight of the package,' the clerk explained.

'What do I do?' asked the Jew.

'Put on more stamps.'

'Are you crazy?' said the Jew, incredulous. 'That will make it even heavier!'

*   *   *   *   *

A waiter in a Jewish restaurant took his family to the zoo on one of his afternoons off and showed his youngest son all the animals. It was feeding time for the tigers when they arrived at their cage, and the little boy watched enthralled as the keepers threw huge lumps of meat to their hungry charges.

As they were walking away the little boy asked his father, 'Papa, why did those men just throw the meat to the tigers instead of serving it nicely like you always do?'

'Just between us,' whispered his father, 'tigers are lousy tippers.'

*   *   *   *   *

'I'm bankrupt,' one businessman confided to another.

'You're not.'

'I am. . . . I tell you, I'm bankrupt.'

'You're bankrupt. . . . You've got some money in the wife's name?'

'No.'

'You've got some money in the safety deposit box?'

'No.'

'You've got some money under the floor-boards?'

'No.'

'You're not bankrupt — you're skint!'

*   *   *   *   *

A woman standing by a gravestone in a cemetery was weeping copiously and wailing, 'Oh, my poor Jack... my poor, poor Jack.'

A man passing by stopped to say gently, 'Excuse me, madam, I think you must be standing by the wrong grave. That stone definitely reads Sarah Rebecca Goldstein.'

'I know,' she said, 'my husband was bankrupt so many times he even put the stone in my name.'

*　　*　　*　　*　　*

Harry Schumacher was giving his wife a driving lesson in their new Mercedes. In fact, she was driving very well. Then, as they reached the top of a very sharp incline, the car began to increase speed rapidly. The car was careering down the other side of the hill.

'Ira, step on the brakes!' yelled Harry.

'I am doing, I think they must be broken!'

'Oh my God, try the emergency brake.'

'It's no good, that's broken too.'

The car was now totally out of control, flying down the hill at a hundred miles an hour. 'What shall I do?' wailed Ira in desperation.

'I don't know,' cried Harry. 'Just hit something cheap!'

*　　*　　*　　*　　*

A rich miser went to the doctor complaining of severe pains in his chest.

'It doesn't look good,' said the doctor gravely. 'However, take this medicine — and if you start to perspire, then all is well. If you don't, I'm afraid that it's time to pray to God.'

So the miser went home and took the medicine. But he didn't perspire. As the days went by, the rumour spread that the old miser was about to die. Soon the rabbi heard the news and decided that, as the man was so near death, he might throw off his old ways and donate some money to the community. So the rabbi visited him with a pen and paper ready to write down any endowments.

'The school is badly in need of repair,' urged the rabbi.

'Write down one hundred pounds for the school,' groaned the miser.

'The paupers' fund could do with some money.'

'A hundred for the paupers!' groaned the miser.

'And the widows, what about them?'

'A hundred for the — wait! Wait!' cried the miser suddenly. 'I'm perspiring, I'm perspiring! Cross it all out!'

*   *   *   *   *

Mr Ginsberg suffered dreadfully from insomnia and believed he had tried all remedies, to no avail. One morning he dragged himself into work and began telling his partner how tired he was and how nothing seemed to cure his sleep-nessness.

'I guess you've tried counting sheep?' asked his partner, without much conviction.

'Of course, the obvious remedy I haven't tried!' cried Mr Ginsberg. 'I'll try tonight.'

The next day, however, he came in looking worse than ever.

'Couldn't sleep?' asked his partner.

'Oy! It's no good! I counted hundreds, then thousands of sheep, and couldn't sleep. I then sheared the sheep, and still couldn't sleep. So, I thought I'd make the wool into overcoats and by the time I'd made a thousand I felt really exhausted and was nearly asleep.'

'So, what went wrong?'

'For the rest of the night I was up worrying. Where could I get a thousand linings?'

*   *   *   *   *

A woman was giving a lecture on sex appeal when, half-way through, a man got up and made to leave.

'What's up?' asked the lecturer. 'Are you offended by what I am saying?'

'Not in the least,' replied the man. 'I thought the part on sex was great — it's just appeals I don't like!'

*   *   *   *   *

It was the time of the Vietnam war and US troops were under pressure when President Nixon met Israel's Prime Minister Golda Meir. They were talking about the fine reputation of the Israeli Army when Nixon said, 'Do you think we could swap generals?'

'Which ones would you want?' asked Golda Meir.

'General Rabin and General Dayan,' said Nixon. 'Which of *our* generals would *you* want?'

'General Motors and General Electric,' replied Golda Meir.

*   *   *   *   *

A Jewish professor was stopped by a student and asked for a donation to his collection 'for the Lord'. The professor asked the student how old he was.

'Twenty-one,' said the young man.

'I'm sixty-five,' said the professor, 'and as I expect to visit the Lord before you I'll give him the donation in person.'

*   *   *   *   *

One Saturday morning a rabbi was walking to the synagogue when he saw one of his flock selling curtains at a stall. 'You should be ashamed of yourself, doing business in front of everyone on the Sabbath,' said the rabbi angrily.

'Rabbi,' replied the salesman, aggrieved, 'I'm losing money on every sale — you call *that* doing business?'

98

Whether through flamboyance or an innate sense of advertising, Jews are seldom backward when it comes to announcing their business qualities and successes to others. They are not shy either in dropping names or capitalizing on the mood of the moment. Necessity, if not always the mother of invention under these circumstances, is certainly the mother of self-advancement.

Most of the money earned for charity shows organized by Jews comes from the sale of the brochure, where high-pressure sales techniques invariably persuade large business houses to place an advertisement for a sizeable sum. The story that always amuses me in connection with this is the one in which an advert is placed wishing success to a particular function followed by the announcement:

Cohen & Marstov,
46 Great Adie Street,
Blouses — Dresses — Skirts — Wholesale and retail
486-7981 (9 lines)
Now showing the latest Spring Collection
(£50 anonymous)

I've Taken a Page in the Bible

The famous banker, Goldie Stein, was driving across town one day, when he noticed a sign displayed above a milliner's shop. It read: 'Benjamin Stein, Cousin of Goldie Stein'.

He was furious that his name was being used in this way, so he stopped the car, and went to see the man responsible.

'I insist that you alter that sign immediately, or I'll inform my lawyers!' he raged.

'Of course, sir,' agreed Benjamin.

The following day, Goldie Stein drove by the shop once again, to see if anything had been done about it. The sign was changed all right. It now read: 'Benjamin Stein, Formerly Cousin of Goldie Stein'.

*   *   *   *   *

Harry and Seymour Kaplan were two brothers who owned shops in the Bronx next door to each other. Harry ran a bookshop; Seymour a delicatessen.

One day Harry placed a sign in his window announcing the current best-seller *All This and Heaven Too*.

The next day Seymour's window had a new sign as well. That read: 'All This and Herring Too'.

*   *   *   *   *

Mendel Sokolov had only arrived in New York the previous summer, and his English still left a lot to be desired. That weekend was Easter, and Mendel was puzzled to hear his gentile neighbours shouting out on Sunday morning: 'Christ has risen! Christ has risen!'

He could not get it out of his mind the whole of the rest of the day. What could they mean? It took many hours of thought, but finally he thought he understood what they meant.

The next day, a sign appeared in Mendel's grocer's shop. It read:

CHRIST HAS RISEN — BUT OUR PRICES REMAIN THE SAME

100

Business is Business

A businessman on a trip to London decided to stay in Harry Koffman's attractive hotel on the edge of the West End. The sign outside read: 'Hotel. Bed and Breakfast. TV.'

As he was preparing to go out that night, the visitor noticed that there was no television in his room.

'Excuse me, Mr Koffman,' he said as he passed the reception area on his way out. 'My room hasn't got a television in it.'

'I know,' replied Harry. 'Did I mention a television set?'

'Yes, you did. The sign outside says quite clearly — TV!'

'No, no,' said Harry. 'What that sign means is "Tourists Velcome".'

*　　　*　　　*　　　*　　　*

Though Hyam Samuelson had made quite a success of his grocery business, it was not until his wife mentioned it that he had ever considered having business cards printed.

'What you need is a card with your name on, so people remember who you are,' she said.

So the next day he went to the printer's to get a batch of cards done. The assistant showed him a number of sample cards, but the one Hyam decided to imitate simply read: Frank Dobson, Iona House, Mayfair.

The copy Hyam submitted to the printer read: Hyam Samuelson, I Own Four Houses, Golders Green.

*　　　*　　　*　　　*　　　*

An Englishman and his wife were on holiday one summer in Israel. Among the many tourist attractions which were on their agenda was the tomb of Israel's unknown soldier. When they arrived at the tomb, they were surprised to see the following inscription: 'Here lies Israel's unknown soldier, Benjamin Freidberg, Silversmith'.

'That's a bit unusual, isn't it?' said the visitor to his guide.

'How can an unknown soldier have a name?'

'Well, you see, sir,' replied the guide, 'as a soldier he *was* unknown, but as a silversmith he was famous!'

* * * * *

An Israeli official was desperately trying to raise the million needed to buy a new jet fighter for the beleaguered air force.

He told a friend that if a thousand wealthy people gave a thousand each, they would have all the money they required to buy the aircraft.

'But the plane would never get off the ground,' his friend objected.

'Why on earth not?' asked the official.

'All those plaques would weigh a ton!'

* * * * *

A rich British Jew was on a tour of his Russian homeland, when he noticed that his watch had stopped. He decided to try to get it repaired in the next village. After searching the place for a while, he finally came across a shop window full of old clocks and watches. When he entered the shop, he noticed a small, greying man, sitting in the corner of the room reading.

'Excuse me,' said the visitor, 'but my watch has stopped. Could you repair it for me straight away, please?'

The man simply shook his head, and carried on reading.

'Did you hear what I said?' continued the visitor, a little annoyed. 'I need my watch repaired.'

Once again, the man shook his head, and returned to his book.

'This is outrageous,' bellowed the visitor. 'Call yourself a watchmaker? You'll never get far in business, if you take this lazy, good-for-nothing attitude!'

'But that's just it,' said the old man finally. 'I'm not a watchmaker.'

'Then what in heaven's name are you?'

'I'm a *mohel*,' replied the man. 'I circumcise the village children.'

'I don't understand,' cried the visitor, angry and perplexed. 'If you're a *mohel*, why do you put all those clocks and watches in your window?'

'Tell me,' said the man, with a smile. 'If you earned your living circumcising babies, what would you put in the window?'

*   *   *   *   *

At one time George Jessel and the actor George Raft owned a travel agency in Los Angeles with a sign in the window that read: 'Please go away.'

*   *   *   *   *

Woody Allen once complained that his apartment had been burgled so many times that he put up a sign that read: 'We gave already.'

*   *   *   *   *

As business partners Jews have always seemed to have a love-hate relationship with each other — they know they can't get along without each other, but how they wish they could!

There's a story of the successful businessman invited to speak to his local Rotary club on business ethics: 'I have been asked to talk to you tonight on business ethics,' he began. 'Now, what exactly are business ethics? I'll give you an example. A lady comes into my shop and buys an article that cost seventy-five pence. She gives me a pound note. What the lady does not know is that there are two pound notes stuck together. Now we come to the ethics. Should I tell my partner?'

In the same vein is an old favourite I enjoy telling about the man who took on a young employee, a bit of a wide boy, and decided he had better keep an eye on him at the start. Hiding behind a curtain in the shop he watched the lad make his first sale and take in a pound. Fifty pence went into the till and fifty into his pocket. The next sale was for thirty pence and the lad divided that with his boss — half for the till, half in his pocket. This went on all day until he made his last sale before closing the shop and pocketed the whole fifty pence. 'What's the matter,' said the boss, coming out from his hiding place, 'we're not partners any more?'

Over the years a mutual respect can develop, of course, and the relationship approaches something like friendship, but the business acumen is never far below the surface.

104

An office junior, returning with his boss's sandwiches and coffee, put them down on the great man's desk and said good-naturedly, 'Isn't this lovely weather we're having?'

'We? All of a sudden you're a partner?'

*   *   *   *   *

Two partners of a firm engaged in the rag trade had left work one evening to attend a dinner which they greatly enjoyed. Suddenly Mr Weizmann's face froze and he gripped his partner's arm.'Arthur,' he gasped, 'I didn't lock the safe before we left the office. I forgot.'

'Don't worry. Relax, enjoy yourself. After all, we're both here!'

*   *   *   *   *

When a new tenant rented an office in a huge tower block, he couldn't help noticing the sign on the office next door to his. It read: 'Goldstein, Finberg, Schwarzbaum, and O'Leary — Accountants'.

He was intrigued, and after a couple of days, he approached the security officer, and asked: 'Listen, I don't want to be nosy, but how on earth did O'Leary get to join the partnership?'

'Easy,' replied the security officer. 'He put up the money!'

*   *   *   *   *

An old stockbroker was lying on his deathbed. His partner was with him, trying desperately to console the poor man. 'Don't worry about it, Manny. God will surely let you live to be a hundred.'

'What are you talking about?' groaned Manny, 'Why should he let me live to be a hundred when he could have me at $82\frac{1}{2}$?'

I've Taken a Page in the Bible

Two immigrant Jews set themselves up in business in New York under their names of Goldberg and Steinberg. However, the business never really got off the ground and, in a desperate effort to improve trade, Goldberg changed his name to O'Brien. Almost overnight things started getting better and soon Steinberg changed his name to O'Brien too.

One day a customer telephoned and asked to speak to Mr O'Brien. 'Which O'Brien do you want?' he was asked. 'Goldberg or Steinberg?'

* * * * *

Lou Stern and Arnie Klein were both tailors in London's Savile Row. One day, while they were having morning coffee, Lou decided he had to get something off his chest.

'Arnie,' he began, 'I know we've been partners a long time, but recently you've been annoying me a little.'

'Annoying you?' said Arnie. 'What are you saying?'

'Well, lately, I feel you've been giving yourself airs. You know what I mean, acting all pretentious.'

'Pretentious?' said Arnie. '*Moi?*'

* * * * *

For many years Abe and Solly worked together successfully in business before branching off into independent enterprises. Many years later Abe went into a run-down café in Whitechapel and recognized his old partner waiting at the tables.

'I don't believe it,' he said when Solly came to his table. 'You, a waiter, in this dump?'

'True,' replied Solly with great dignity. 'But I don't eat here.'

* * * * *

106

One of the most successful Broadway partnerships was that between George S. Kaufman and his fellow playwright Moss Hart. Where Kaufman was cautious about the way he spent his money, Hart relished grand, extravagant gestures. When he visited Hart in the country once and saw with amazement the extensive landscaping that was taking place in his grounds, Kaufman commented, 'This is what God would have done if he'd had the money.'

On another occasion he explained why he liked working with Hart, who seemed to bring the partnership good luck, 'I like to be near you, Moss. It comes under the heading of *gelt* by association.'

Moss Hart was commissioned to write the screenplay of *Gentleman's Agreement*, Laura Hobson's novel against anti-semitism, which, in 1947, became the first of a series of anti-racialist films produced in Hollywood. He asked Kaufman if he liked the book. 'I don't have to pay three dollars fifty to find out what it feels like to be a Jew,' answered his partner sourly.

*   *   *   *   *

A man walked into the offices of a dress firm in Whitechapel and asked the receptionist, 'Is Mr Goldberg in?'

'I'm sorry,' she replied, 'Mr Goldberg is in America.'

'Is Mr Levi in?'

'Mr Levi is in Puerto Rico.'

'Is Mr Levine here?'

'Mr Levine is in Paris.'

'Is Mr Goldman in?'

'Mr Goldman is tied up.'

'Really?'

'Yes — whenever Mr Goldberg is in America, Mr Levi is in Puerto Rico and Mr Levine is in Paris, we always tie up Mr Goldman.'

Another dominant characteristic seen among Jews, and certainly in their business dealings, is the doctrine of 'Don't mix in'. It's the ability to stick to your own interest and let the other fellow worry about his troubles. Again this is a quality that has been instilled into the Jewish personality through hundreds of years of persecution and struggle, and from it springs that quality of dismissive practicality that brings us back to the pragmatic business sense we started with.

The night the *Titanic* hit an iceberg, chaos broke out among the passengers. A few lifeboats were available, but not nearly enough to accommodate all the people on the ship. Everyone was rushing up and down, frantically searching for some sort of life-preserver to protect them against the ravages of the sea below. Children cried uncontrollably, and women screamed hysterically. Some people couldn't stand all the waiting around, and simply jumped overboard. Others just sat in corners, desperately cursing their luck.

Only one person among the passengers was calm — Manny Crockelstein.

When the captain noticed Manny calmly playing solitaire patience in the bar, while pandemonium raged around him, he couldn't believe his eyes. 'Are you insane?' he yelled. 'Don't you realize that the ship is sinking?'

'Yes,' replied Manny nonchalantly, 'but that's no reason for me to get excited. After all, do I own the ship?'

* * * * *

A party of Jewish businessmen from the East End decided to take themselves off on a big game hunt in India.

Deep in the heart of the jungle one of the native bearers hurried back to them and said to one of the hunters, '*Sahib*... *sahib*... fifty yards ahead... big tiger.'

'Don't tell me. Tell Hymie, he's the furrier.'

* * * * *

A Jewish tailor looking for someone to manage his accounts interviewed a fellow Jew who boasted some experience of book-keeping, and asked him, 'See if you can work this out for me quickly. How much would a pair of trousers cost if I used one and a quarter yards of material costing two pounds ten a yard, and paid five pounds for labour?'

'What's the use of figures like that?' asked the would-be book-keeper. 'An intelligent person would know what to do.'

'Would he? What's that, then?'

'He'd buy a ready-made pair of trousers.'

* * * * *

A Jewish businessman knew he was about to die so he asked his rabbi to give him a hand in making his will.

'I want to leave my business to Rachel, my daughter,' said the businessman.

'Be careful,' said the rabbi, 'running a firm might be too much for an inexperienced young woman; perhaps you should leave it to one of your sons.'

Undeterred, the businessman said he wanted to leave half a million pounds to his third son, who was still at university.

Again the rabbi advised caution, saying that was too much money for such an inexperienced youth.

Finally, the businessmen said he would give some land to his youngest son, who was still only a schoolboy.

'Be careful,' warned the rabbi once more. 'He may be too young to cope with the responsibility.'

'Now just tell me, rabbi,' said the man, exasperated, 'who is dying — you or me?'

*   *   *   *   *

It was the Day of Atonement, the most solemn day of the year. The synagogue was packed as usual and admission was by ticket only. Outside stood the beadle checking the congregation as they arrived, when a man rushed up to the crowd and tried to squeeze inside.

'Wait a moment, where are you going?' shouted the beadle.

'I've got to see my partner for one moment. It's very important. It's...'

'Sorry. Have you got a ticket?'

'No,' said the man, 'I haven't got a ticket, but I have to see my partner...'

'Sorry,' said the beadle. 'No ticket, no entry.'

'But I only want to see him for a minute. I've got to get his signature on a cheque. That's all I need. Otherwise we stand to lose a hundred thousand pounds.'

'You got a ticket?'

'No, I haven't. But I only want to see him for five seconds. Are you going to let me in?'

'All right. I'll let you in... but if I catch you praying...'

*   *   *   *   *

A Jewish refugee arrived in Britain looking for work. He heard that there might be a job going at a Jewish community

110

as the *shamus*, so he went to see the leader. They discussed the vacancy for a while and then the refugee asked what his exact duties would be as sexton. The leader said he would have to make sure the synagogue was ready for services, give out prayer books — and issue receipts for donations.

'I'm sorry,' said the Jew, 'I'm afraid I never learned to read or write.'

'I'm sorry, then, but we can't take you on — a *shamus* needs to be able to read and write,' replied the president.

The Jew went off, disheartened. However, a little while later he had a stroke of luck. A wealthy friend of his advanced him a small sum of money with which he bought some goods and started selling on the streets. Within a year he had done so well he was able to buy his own store.

Within two years he was thriving and in a position to open more stores. So he went to his bank manager and asked for a loan of £70,000.

'No problem,' the manager replied, 'just sign this bit of paper.'

'But I don't know how to write,' said the refugee.

The bank manager was astonished. 'Do you know what you could be today if you had learnt to read and write?'

'Yes,' replied the Jew, 'a *shamus*.'

*   *   *   *   *

A man who needed a new pair of trousers for an impending holiday went to his local tailor to be measured.

'That's all, sir,' said the tailor, putting his tape-measure away. 'I'll have them ready for you in four days.'

Four days later, the man returned.

'I'm sorry, sir,' said the tailor, 'I've made a mess of the seat. Come back next week.'

A week later, the man returned.

'Forgive me,' said the tailor, 'but your trousers are still not ready. You'll have to come back after your holiday.'

The man was furious, but realized that it was no use arguing. He returned to the tailor on the day he got back from holiday, four weeks later.

'You'll never believe it,' said the tailor, 'but I've had a lot of trouble with the flies. Come back tomorrow, and they'll be perfect.'

The man couldn't hold back his anger any longer. 'For God's sake, man, this is too much, too much! Six days, I repeat six days, it took the Almighty to create the whole world. *The world, I say!* Yet you are not capable of making a simple pair of trousers in six weeks!'

'Please, sir, please,' replied the tailor. 'You're being unfair. I mean, look at the mess God made of the world — and then look at my *lovely* trousers!'

*   *   *   *   *

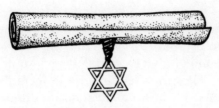

The Jew's obsession with business matters can eclipse every other consideration, as this piece from the story It's Never Too Late *by Montague Glass illustrates. Glass was a popular US humourist and short story writer whose collections* Potash *and* Perlmutter *and* Abe *and* Mawruss *became stage successes.*

This scene could be transferred on to the stage almost as it stands, to create a brilliantly funny business confrontation between the patient who's trying to clinch a deal with the doctor treating him, without letting his temporary incapacitation blunt his sharp business edge.

To fill in the background, Uncle Harris has been taken suddenly ill (in his own words 'It was borscht *(beetroot soup) I ett at Wasserbrauer's last week!') and has staggered into a hotel in New York groaning in agony, where the hotel doctor has been called to a room to treat him.*

'Is there anything I can do for you?' the hotel doctor asked.

'Send for the doctor, quick,' Uncle Harris moaned.

'But I am a doctor,' the hotel doctor explained.

'Don't argue with me,' Uncle Harris said. 'I want a doctor, not a hotel doctor.'

He waved his right hand weakly.

'Ring up Dr Sigmund Eichendorfer,' he said. 'He's in the telephone book, and he wouldn't let me die — not till I bought them two walk-ups from him anyhow.

'And if he ain't in, Dr Koppel Polongin would do,' Harris said, faintly. 'He's got a half interest in them flats.'

The manner in which the hotel doctor administered one half a grain of morphine to Uncle Harris's fat arm was a model of professional outraged dignity, even if he did jab Uncle Harris pretty savagely with the hypodermic needle. After that he busied himself laying the foundation for a charge of a hundred dollars by sending out a bellboy to the nearest drug store and buying, at Uncle Harris's expense, enough ice bags and other India rubber products to make Harris's room look as though it were the surgical supply department of a corner chain drug store. Nor did Dr Sigmund Eichendorfer arrive for more than two hours, since it had been necessary for his office nurse to telephone to four poker games and a pinochle party before she could notify him of Harris Gittelberg's plight, and so urgent had the case been made out to be that Doctor Eichendorfer had left for Harris's hotel after only two rounds of consolations. He quickly decided, upon examining Harris, that three rounds might have been fatal to the patient.

'Well, boss,' he said to Harris, palpitating both sides of his patient's highly sensitive body, 'I guess you ain't got much to worry about. Leave it to me and you'll be on the table in half an hour.'

After telephoning to Mount Hebron Hospital for an ambulance, he turned to the hotel doctor.

'This is his second attack to my knowledge,' he explained. 'The first one occurred about a week ago. Would you care to hear a brief history of it?'

The hotel doctor nodded, while Doctor Eichendorfer cleared his throat impressively.

'He came up to see me direct from a luncheon appointment he had filled, and we went round together to see two apartment houses of mine on One Hundred and Twenty-fourth Street,' Doctor Eichendorfer began.

'What do you mean — apartment houses?' Harris protested, weakly. 'They was cold-water walk-ups, and not even stair carpets.'

'I told you at the time I intended to put in stair carpet, and I have all the plans and specifications for installing a hot-water supply for nine hundred dollars,' Doctor Eichendorfer said.

'I know them nine-hundred-dollar hot-water supplies,' Uncle Harris moaned. 'They don't give hot water. All they give is excuses for tenants to break their leases,' he added, bitterly.

'About what did Mr Gittelberg complain at the time?' the hotel doctor inquired.

'I complained about everything,' Uncle Harris volunteered, in feeble tones. 'The lots was only twenty-three-six by a hundred foot eleven, instead of twenty-five, as him and that feller Polongin claimed, and there was two violations on the buildings for fire escapes, and water in the cellar.'

'The violations could have been removed at any time,' Doctor Eichendorfer said, 'and don't waste your strength by talking. You're in a bad way.'

'I would be in a worse way if I had took them flats in the state they're in,' Uncle Harris said, 'and, anyhow, eighteen thousand five hundred apiece is just a thousand too much for them.'

'That's our price,' Eichendorfer said, firmly, 'or, anyhow, eighteen thousand two hundred and fifty, all cash above the first mortgage.'

Uncle Harris raised himself groaning on one elbow.

'Listen, Doctor,' he said, 'you want to sell them cold-water walk-ups and I want to buy them, ain't it?'

'How can you talk this way in your condition?' the hotel doctor protested.

'Never mind my condition,' Uncle Harris said. 'The

115

ambulance wouldn't be here for five minutes yet, so I tell you what I'll do, Eichendorfer. I'll buy them flats from you, no stair carpets, violations, and everything, for eighteen thousand two hundred fifty all cash above the first mortgage, and you will throw in them tools and step-ladders in the basement and also any and all necessary operating which you've got to do on me for this trouble of mine.'

'Make it eighteen thousand four hundred and it's a deal,' Eichendorfer said. 'And I'll ring up Polongin, he should administer the anaesthetic, which will make it eighteen thousand three hundred flat.'

A loud clanging in the street outside punctuated the pause which ensued, and Uncle Harris sank back exhausted on his pillow.

'Done!' he whispered, as the ambulance attendant knocked on the door. 'And this here hotel doctor is a witness.'

*   *   *   *   *

How do you want your 'no', fast or slow?

Michael Todd

*   *   *   *   *

Fritters in a dream are not fritters, but a dream.

Sholom Aleichem

*   *   *   *   *

You should have a lot of money, but you should be the only one in your family with it.

Ernst Lubitsch, his own version of a Jewish curse

*   *   *   *   *

If it isn't a Stradivarius, I've been robbed of a hundred and ten dollars.

Jack Benny, on his violin

116

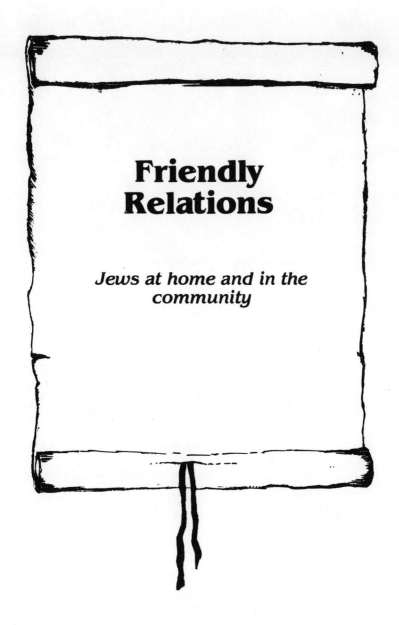

Friendly Relations

Jews at home and in the community

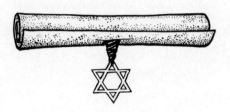

The family holds a position of great importance for the Jew and at the centre of the family is the Jewish mother, devoting herself body and soul to the well-being of her offspring. She is unique, allowing herself to become so wrapped up in her family that reason and commonsense come a very poor second.

When I was thirty-five we were living in Clapton at eighty-three Ickburgh Road, and while I was doing a television show I was nabbed for speeding – a nothing offence, but enough to get my name in the paper. Unfortunately the tiny line in the Evening Standard *that reported this got the numbers mixed up and announced that, 'Eighty-five-year-old Alfred Marks of thirty-three Ickburgh Road was convicted of speeding'. My mother came in, white as a sheet, asking, 'Have you seen this? How dare they! How dare they print this!', which I thought was very considerate of her, not that it bothered me in the slightest. And while I was there she got on to the editor of the* Evening Standard *and demanded, 'What's the meaning of this? How old does that make me?'*

In his autobiography A Poet in the Family, *Dannie Abse, the Welsh poet, doctor and brother of MP Leo Abse, quotes a delightful example of the concern for her children by the archetypal Jewish mother:*

My mother was busy telling Joan how some months earlier she had called into Lear's bookshop in Cardiff to enquire how my book of poems was selling. 'I asked how is my son's book selling and the assistant asked, "Who is your son, madam?" So naturally I said Dannie Abse and do you know what he said?'

'No,' said Joan.

'He said "Not as well as Dylan Thomas's *Collected Poems*, madam, which has also recently been published." So I told him "My son," I said, "my son is the *Welsh* Dylan Thomas."''

* * * * *

Mrs Nandelbaum was taking her young granddaughter for a walk in the park, when she happened to bump into her friend, Mrs Ginsberg.

'Oh, what a beautiful little girl,' trilled Mrs Ginsberg.

'Why, thank you,' replied Mrs Nandelbaum, 'but this is nothing. You should see her photographs!'

* * * * *

'My daughter married a man in computers,' one Jewish matron boasted to another. 'You know, he makes so much money they have four cars!'

'Do they have any children?' asked the other. 'My daughter has two sets of twins.'

'They have a little boy — fifteen months old.'

'And does he walk yet? All my grandchildren were walking very early.'

'With four cars, why should he walk?!'

*   *   *   *   *

A Jewish woman whose son had just been called up by the US army during the war was walking along the street loudly denouncing the President for 'taking my boy'. A fellow Jew rushed up to her. 'Be careful,' he warned, 'if the police hear you denouncing the President they will arrest you.'

The woman stopped, for with three other children to support she could not afford to be thrown into gaol. 'Then can I denounce the President's wife?' she asked.

Her companion considered for a moment. 'I think so,' he said, 'she's just a private citizen.'

'Please Almighty,' she shouted, 'make her a widow!'

*   *   *   *   *

The story goes that the American entertainer, George Jessel, eagerly telephoned his mother with the news that he had just bought a Rubens.

'Rubin? Rubin the delicatessen man?'

'No, Mama, Rubens is a painter,' he explained tactfully.

'Oh, this I didn't know,' she said breathlessly. 'Listen Georgie, ask how much he'll charge to paint the kitchen.'

*   *   *   *   *

There's a story that immediately after signing a film contract for a million dollars, Kirk Douglas phoned his mother to tell her the news. 'Ma, I've made it,' he exclaimed. 'I've done it! I've just signed a contract for a million dollars! How about that?'

121

'Son,' she replied, 'I just saw your new movie. You should eat more. You look a bit skinny in it.'

*   *   *   *   *

Out walking one day, Mrs Finkelstein met Mrs Bernstein who was pushing her two little boys in a pram.

'*Oy*... such beautiful boys!' exclaimed Mrs Finkelstein, 'and how old are these *boychiklech* now?'

With great pride Mrs Bernstein replied, 'The doctor is two, and the lawyer is one, already.'

*   *   *   *   *

Mrs Mendelsohn could not contain herself when she met her friend Mrs Ginsberg. 'My son Simon is seeing a psychiatrist,' she said.

Not sure what to say, her friend replied, 'My dear, I am sorry.'

'Sorry, nothing!' Mrs Mendelsohn said eagerly. 'Do you know he goes twice a week, and pays seventy dollars a time, and all he does is talk about me.'

*   *   *   *   *

Sadie Heschel was recovering in hospital after performing the feat of producing triplets. Her mother-in-law came to see her and to marvel. 'No one on our side of the family ever had triplets, as far as I know,' she said.

'Well,' said her daughter-in-law rather smugly, 'the doctors say it only happens once in a million times.'

'Oh! Sadie, when did you manage to do the housework?'

*   *   *   *   *

When the first American was rocketed into space the nation followed his progress, few more enthusiastically than a little Jewish boy in the Bronx.

'Mom! Mom!' he shouted running into the kitchen. 'Do you know, John Glenn's already gone round the world forty-one times?'

'So?' said his mother, without looking up from her saucepan. 'If you have the money, you can travel.'

*   *   *   *   *

An old Jewish lady entered a delicatessen one day, and told the proprietor that she wanted some salami.

'Which one would you like, madam?' asked the proprietor.

The woman pointed to the longest salami in the shop, and said, 'Cut me some slices of that.'

After he had cut about a dozen slices, he asked if that was enough.

'No, keep cutting.'

The proprietor shrugged his shoulders and carried on cutting. When he had got about a quarter of the way through the salami, he once again asked if it was enough.

Again the same reply: 'Keep on cutting.'

Thinking that the woman must be catering for quite a party of people, he went on cutting. When he reached the middle, the woman suddenly shouted, 'Stop! That's enough. Now, from the middle, cut me about a half a dozen slices!'

*   *   *   *   *

Mischa Elman's prodigious musical talent was apparent in his childhood, and he used to enjoy telling the story of the time when he played for guests of family friends at the age of seven. He began with Beethoven's 'Kreutzer' sonata, which has several long rest intervals. During one of these pauses an elderly lady leaned across and whispered comfortingly, 'Why don't you play something you know, darling?'

123

The Finsberg family were gathered together to hear the last will and testament of Abel Finsberg.

'I, Abel Finsberg,' began the lawyer, 'being of sound mind and body, do bequeath my wordly goods as follows: To my lovely wife Mabel, who cooked and washed for me, who bore me two lovely children, who was my companion throughout my life, I leave one million dollars.'

'What a wonderful man,' said a relative.

'And to my loyal son, Hymie, who was always obedient, and became a doctor like I wanted, and didn't smoke or drink too much, I leave half a million dollars.'

'Marvellous! So generous!'

'And to my daughter Jayne, who is very beautiful like her mother, and if she wasn't so choosy might be married already, I also leave half a million dollars.'

'What a man!'

'And to my younger brother Zachary, who never gave me a minute's peace, who gambled and womanized while I worked hard, who was a disgrace to our parents, Zachary, who asked me a number of times during my last few days on earth to remember him in my will... Hello Zachary!'

*   *   *   *   *

'And how is Nancy doing at school?' Mr Henkel asked his wife.

'Not too good, Papa,' she replied. 'She keeps getting these detentions. I don't know what to do.'

'What for?'

'Same thing — she couldn't remember where the Himalayas are.'

Mr Henkel sighed. 'Last week she couldn't remember where the Dardanelles were. Now she can't find the Himalayas! I just don't understand it. I mean I keep telling her. I say, "Nancy, you've got to remember where you put things!"'

124

Friendly Relations

As an old Jew lay on his death bed he overheard his two sons in the next room discussing the funeral arrangements.

'Let's hire a fleet of Rolls Royces for the mourners,' said Arnie.

'Are you crazy?' said Isaac. 'That would cost us a fortune — we'll hire one and the rest of the mourners can go by private car.'

'OK,' said Arnie, 'but let's order forty wreaths for the service.'

'Are you out of your mind?' said Isaac, 'that's far too extravagant — we can make do with a couple.'

Suddenly the two heard their father's voice. 'Isaac,' said the old man weakly, 'will you fetch my clothes?'

'No, Dad, you know you must stay in bed,' said the son.

'But, Isaac,' said his father, 'I want to walk to the cemetery — it will save you hiring a hearse!'

*   *   *   *   *

A young man, newly arrived in town, emerged from the railway station, and went in search of a taxi. As he was waiting at the nearest taxi-rank, he turned to the prosperous-looking man in front of him and asked, 'Do you have the right time, please?'

The old man looked him up and down for a few seconds, and replied, 'Go to Hell!'

The young man was shocked, but most of all, he was angry. 'What's your problem?' he cried. 'I only asked you a perfectly civil question. There's no need to be so rude.'

At first the old man tried to ignore him, but the young man repeated his demand. 'Come on, what's your problem?' he said.

'Okay, if you insist, I'll tell you,' replied the old man at last. 'First you ask me a simple question, and, all right, suppose I answer you? Then what? You start a conversation about the weather, about business, about politics. Then religion comes

125

up, and we find that we're both Jews. Now it's started. You're new in town, a stranger, so I must offer you some traditional Jewish hospitality, and invite you back for supper. What next? You meet my lovely daughter Caroline, of course, and after a few more visits to my house, you fall in love with each other. And before I know it you're asking my permission to get married. Believe me, my son, by telling you to go to Hell, I'm saving you a lot of trouble. Because I can assure you that I would never allow my daughter to marry a man who can't even afford his own watch!'

* * * * *

One Jew asked another Jew if he would rather have ten million pounds or ten daughters. The second Jew thought for a while and replied, 'Ten daughters.'

'How so?' asked the first Jew.

'Well, if I had ten million pounds,' said the second, 'I would still want more — but not if I had ten daughters!'

* * * * *

Two Jews were talking about relatives. 'My son-in-law is useless,' said one. 'He can't gamble and he can't drink.'

'But surely,' said his friend, 'that's a good thing.'

'Not really,' replied the father-in-law. 'He still does both!'

* * * * *

Worried about the sort of girls her son was going out with, an old-fashioned Jewish mother went through the boy's pockets. She found a make-up case on which was written 'Helena Rubinstein'.

'Thank God for that,' said the mother, 'at least this girlfriend's Jewish!'

'Papa,' said the doting mother, 'Issy's teacher says he should have an enyclopedia.'

'Encylopedia, nothing,' grumbled Papa. 'Let him walk to school like I did.'

*   *   *   *   *

Even if the shadchen *does not carry the authority and responsibility he once did, concern over the right marriage is still great enough to give Jewish parents sleepless nights and ulcers.*

However, Jewish marriages usually end up no better and no worse than any others. The close confines of a Jewish family just tend to act as a crucible for all the underlying characteristics of the race, which can heighten tensions and exaggerate domestic discord. There is intense devotion, complete irrationality, utter loathing — the complete spectrum of human emotions squeezed into the closest human bond.

The very wealthy Mrs Levine was attending a charity ball and, to her gratification, was soon surrounded by an admiring — and rather envious — group of ladies.

'Yes,' she said with affected unconcern, 'they are beautiful diamonds, the Levine diamonds. It is unfortunate that they carry the Levine curse.'

'What's that?' asked one of the circle round her.

'Mr Levine.'

*   *   *   *   *

Friendly Relations

Papa came home from work and found his daughter crying her eyes out. 'It's Mama,' she wailed, 'she keeps pestering me to get married when I don't want to.'

Papa promised to talk to Mama, and that night after they had gone to bed, he whispered to her, 'Do me a favour, will you? Leave Rosie alone. She's young yet. Let her wait till the right man comes along.'

'Why should *she* wait so long?' asked Mama. 'I didn't when I was her age.'

*   *   *   *   *

Saul and his wife Rachel came to see their rabbi one day to discuss the bad state of their marriage.

'It's terrible, rabbi,' complained Saul. 'My wife never stops attacking me, calling me all the worst names on earth! I think I want a divorce.'

The rabbi was keen that the couple should stay together, so he suggested a solution to the problem.

'Listen to me, Rachel,' said the rabbi. 'Whenever you wish to curse your husband, think again. Instead of saying "You swine", say "You wonderful man". That way your marriage will be peaceful once more.'

Rachel gave the rabbi her word that she would do as he advised, and the couple left. A few days later, as they were eating their evening meal, Rachel became extremely annoyed by the way Saul was slurping his soup. She was about to attack him, when she remembered her promise to the rabbi.

'Saul,' she said, after a moment's pause, 'I think you're a wonderful man — but you know what I mean!'

*   *   *   *   *

'Is there anything wrong, Mrs Cohen?' asked a friend. 'You look awful.'

129

'Yes... it's the same as always. My husband is ill again.'
'He's just a hypochondriac. He isn't really ill. He only thinks he's ill.'

A month passed, and the two friends met again. Mrs Cohen looked worse than ever.

'Is he any better?' asked her friend.

'Worse,' Mrs Cohen replied. 'He thinks he's dead.'

* * * * *

Mrs Rosen met her neighbour Mrs Gold while she was out shopping one day. 'Have you met the woman who's just moved in across the road?' asked Mrs Rosen. 'She's terrible.'

'Oh, you mean the one who's always going on about her husband?'

'Going on about him? Believe me, it's worse than that. She complains about him non-stop, to anyone who'll listen. Now, I know my husband doesn't attend synagogue like he should. And yes, he drinks too much, and gambles, and sometimes I wish he would just drop dead! But I don't go around telling everyone about it!'

* * * * *

Moses' brother, Aaron, was furious when he heard that Pharaoh had again broken his promise to release the children of Israel from their bondage in Egypt.

When he got home to his wife that night, he couldn't control his venom any longer. 'I tell you, this Pharaoh, he really is a *momzer* — he's a real bastard!'

'Aaron, please,' said his wife, 'there's no need for language like that. Remember that we are all the children of God. Each of us is descended from the same family, begun by Adam and Eve — even Pharaoh.'

'You are right, my wife,' admitted Aaron, 'but that Pharaoh, he must be from *your* side of the family!'

Mrs Nathan was appearing before the court in a divorce action.

'How old are you?' asked the judge.

'Thirty,' replied Mrs Nathan.

The judge looked surprised. Mrs Nathan certainly looked older. 'Would you mind showing me your birth certificate, please?' he asked.

Mrs Nathan handed the document over, and the judge looked at it for a few moments. 'But, Mrs Nathan,' he said gravely, 'according to your birth certificate, you are fifty.'

'That's right, your honour,' replied Mrs Nathan calmly, 'but the last twenty years I've spent with my husband I'm not counting. I mean, do you call that living?'

*   *   *   *   *

When her husband was promoted to sales manager, Mrs Bagelbaum was determined to celebrate in some way. Finally she decided to do something to improve their garden. That way the neighbours would realize that they had gone up in the world. So she went to the local Garden Centre for some advice.

'I can't decide what to do to make my garden look beautiful,' she moaned.

'Perhaps madam should have a border?' suggested the proprietor.

'What are you talking about?' snapped Mrs Bagelbaum. 'My husband's just been made sales manager. Who needs a boarder?'

*   *   *   *   *

A middle-aged Jewish couple were walking by a river when the husband slipped and fell in. Fortunately, he was fished out before going under for the last time, but he was in pretty poor shape by the time of the rescue. The small crowd gathered on the bank offered advice and one was heard to say, 'Give him artificial respiration!'

Hearing this, the expensively-dressed wife looked really agitated and exclaimed, 'Not artificial respiration! Real respiration or nothing!'

*   *   *   *   *

There was a knock on the door and a man came into the room where Mrs Cohen was slurping her hot chicken soup, the Jewish mother's panacea for every ill from a cut finger to cancer.

'Mrs Cohen?' he asked hesitantly.

'Yes,' she replied, continuing to slurp her soup.

'I've got some bad news for you...'

'Yes,' still slurping the soup.

'Your husband Morrie has had an accident. He got caught up in a machine at the workshop and he's dead.'

Mrs Cohen carried on slurping her soup.

'Madam, I've just told you that your husband's dead.'

'I heard you. When I've finished this soup, I'm going to let out such a scream!'

*   *   *   *   *

Old Goldstein's health didn't seem to be getting any better, so his wife decided that a trip to Miami would do him some good. Unfortunately, after a couple of weeks sitting in the Florida sunshine, he died.

A week later, the whole family gathered for the funeral.

As they stood round the coffin to pay their last respects, his son said, 'I must say, he looks great.'

'Yes,' agreed Goldstein's wife. 'I think those two weeks in Miami did him the world of good.'

*   *   *   *   *

An old Jewish lady went to a photographer who specialized in restoration, and handed him a faded sepia photograph of her dead husband. 'Do you think you can copy this?' she asked.

'Yes, we can.'

'It's very faded.'

'That doesn't matter, we can get the colour back.'

'It's a very old-fashioned photograph. That stand-up collar, can you do something about that?'

'We can make it look like a modern collar.'

'Oh thank you... and that suit? The lapels are very narrow.'

'That doesn't matter. We can get a retouch artist to make them look a bit wider.'

'His hat, that's very old-fashioned too. Can you take the hat away?'

'Yes, the retouch artist can paint the hat out. Which side did your husband part his hair?'

'When you take his hat off you'll see, won't you?' she answered in amazement.

* * * * *

As usual, Sid and Edith were arguing.

'Okay, okay,' admitted Edith at last, 'so I enjoy spending money. But name one other extravagance.'

* * * * *

A Jewish judge was deciding a divorce case. 'Are your relations really unsatisfactory?' he asked the woman.

'Mine are OK,' said the woman, 'it's my husband's who are the problem!'

Given the Jewish mother, it isn't surprising that Jewish husbands find the Jewish mother-in-law an uphill battle.

They can show great devotion to the institution of marriage none the less. I enjoy the story of the man who went to a friend because his firm was sending him away for a week and asked him to take care of his wife. 'We've been together for ten years and never been apart,' he explained, 'she's very nervous. We haven't got any kids and I know she'll fret while I'm away. Do me a favour, will you? Here's fifty quid. Tell her you're my friend and take her out.'

When he got back from the trip they met up and the husband asked if everything had gone all right. 'I'd better tell you the truth,' his friend began, 'it's very serious, you see. I went round to your flat, like you said. She's a smashing girl your wife, a lovely looker. I told her I was a friend of yours and told her you'd given me fifty quid to take her out. So we went up town and saw a show, had some supper and came back to your place. On the doorstep I said "good night", but she asked me in for a coffee and a brandy, and while we were having these she showed me round. She showed me the bedroom. We had another brandy as we sat on the edge of the bed talking. Then after another brandy we sort of found ourselves undressed. We had another brandy and before we knew what we were doing we were in bed

*together and getting down to it. But when we realized what
we'd done, we sat on the edge of that bed and we cried.
Hymie, did we cry! And that's how it's been all the week —
sex and cry, cry and sex, sex and cry . . . '*

*You want to know what Jewish husbands are like?
That's what Jewish husbands are like — and that's what
Jewish husbands' friends are like!*

———————

When her beloved husband Sol died of a heart attack, his wife
Rachel was grief-stricken. She was also a strong believer in
the powers of spiritualism. For months she went to various
different seances, in the hope of making contact with Sol.
Then, one day, she decided to try a new approach.

'I know,' she said. 'Sol was a waiter all his adult life. He
even died on the job. If I can hold a séance in his old
restaurant, he's sure to return from the world of spirits.'

So she telephoned the manager of Sol's restaurant, and,
after pleading with him for a while, finally managed to
persuade him to let her hold a séance there. That night, with
a few friends, she entered the restaurant and sat at a table.

'Sol, are you there?' she said after they had all held hands.

'Hello there, Rachel,' came the immediate reply. It was
Sol, sure enough. Rachel was overjoyed, but his voice was a
little faint.

'Can you speak up a bit, darling, I can hardly hear you.'

'This is the loudest I get.'

'Then come a little closer, you fool.'

'I can't, Rachel, you should know that.'

'Why on earth not?'

'Because that's not my table!'

I've Taken a Page in the Bible

Mr Goldberg returned home after a really terrible day at the office, and collapsed into his favourite chair. Before he could say anything, Mrs Goldberg began her customary monologue of complaints about her day.

'Sarah,' groaned Mr Goldberg, 'Sarah, please don't you start. Why not ask what sort of day I've had? Go on, ask me for once.'

'So what sort of a day did you have?' asked his wife, made nervous by her husband's manner.

'What sort of a day? Better, maybe, you don't ask.'

* * * * *

At the end of a detailed lecture, during which he had outlined his quantum theory and various speculations concerning relativity, Albert Einstein returned glumly to his study.

Noticing this, one of his fellow professors followed him in. 'You spoke brilliantly just now. What possible reason can you have for looking so down in the mouth?'

'Reason enough,' Einstein told him. 'My wife doesn't understand me.'

* * * * *

Two business friends, Feldman and Finkelbaum, went out for a drink after work one night. What was originally planned as just a quick throat-wetter turned into a night on the tiles. They drank until closing time, then went on to a nightclub. When they emerged from the club at three in the morning, Feldman suddenly looked terrified.

'What am I going to do? My wife made it quite clear that I was to be back at eight sharp for dinner.'

'For God's sake, Feldman,' slurred his friend. 'Don't be a wimp, act like a man.'

'Oh, wonderful,' cried Feldman. 'Here I am deep in trouble and he wants me to do an impersonation!'

A very naïve and very orthodox Jewish couple went to see their doctor. 'Doctor, we've been married for two years,' said the husband, 'and we haven't got any children.'

'I see,' replied the doctor. 'Well, what position do you use?'
'Position?'
'Yes, when you're having sex.'
'Sex?'
'When you're making love.'
'Love?'
'Yes... well, what do you do when you go to bed?'
'We hold hands. I kiss her on the cheek, and we go to sleep.'
'That's it? Well, how do you think children happen?'
'You marry and God in his wisdom gives you children.'

'No, no it doesn't happen like that,' said the doctor wearily, realizing that the only way to get the message across was to give a practical demonstration. 'Would you mind taking your clothes off and lying on that examination table,' he said to the girl. Then he stripped off and showed the husband what he ought to be doing in bed. 'Now she'll need that at least twice a week,' he explained as he was getting dressed.

'Well, I can bring her Wednesday and Fridays,' said the husband.

*   *   *   *   *

Milton Cohen arrived home as usual one evening from a day at the office, but, strangely enough, his wife wasn't there to greet him.

'Dar-ling, my dar-ling,' he cooed. 'Where are you?'
The reply was equally playful. 'I'm hiding.'
'Dar-ling, my dar-ling, I've got a little present for you. Where are you?'
Again the same reply. 'I'm hiding.'
'Dar-ling, my dar-ling, it's a lovely surprise. Where are you?'
'I'm hiding.'

137

'Dar-ling, my dar-ling, it's that gold bracelet you wanted. Where are you?'

'I'm hiding — under the stairs!'

*   *   *   *   *

While on holiday in Africa, a Jewish family visited a game reserve to see the wildlife. The mother-in-law went off on her own, unnoticed, until her daughter suddenly saw her standing face to face with a lion.

'Oh my God!' cried the daughter. 'What are we going to do?'

'Nothing,' replied the husband. 'The lion got himself into this mess, so let him get out of it!'

*   *   *   *   *

When his mother-in-law died, it fell to George to deal with all the funeral arrangements. At the undertaker's the following day, George was asked how he wanted to dispose of the body.

'You have three choices — you can have her buried, cremated, or embalmed,' said the undertaker.

George thought about it for a while. 'Look,' he said finally. 'Why take any chances? Do all three!'

*   *   *   *   *

When it comes to getting along with people outside the family, the Jew is generally pretty gregarious. Just occasionally the shutters come down when people start taking an advantage, but on the whole Jews enjoy company; and among Jewish matrons there's a fine tradition of scoring useful social points at gatherings ranging from canasta parties to wedding receptions.

One Jewish lady, to another, meeting by chance in a hotel lobby, 'Darling! Wonderful to see you. You look marvellous, what have you been doing?'

Her friend replies, 'Well, it's a secret, really, but you I'll tell. I'm having an affair.'

'Really? So who's catering?'

*   *   *   *   *

'My doctor told me I really should have another operation,' a Jewish matron told her friends at one of their regular get-togethers. 'But we've had so many expenses this year that I had to tell him I just couldn't afford it.'

'Never mind,' consoled one of her friends, 'so you'll have to talk about your old operation for another year.'

*   *   *   *   *

I've Taken a Page in the Bible

The Ginsbergs had just returned from their European vacation and were enthusing about it, at length, to their neighbours.

'And guess what,' said Mr Ginsberg, 'when we were in Rome we had an audience with the Pope!'

'Really?' said his friends, somewhat amazed. 'So what was he like?'

Mrs Ginsberg gushed, '*He* was charming. *Her*, I didn't take to.'

* * * * *

A woman sitting on a bus turned to the young man next to her and said, 'Hello.'

'Hello,' he replied uncertainly.

'You don't recognize me, do you?'

'No.'

'You don't recognize *me*?'

'Sorry.'

'When I tell you who I am you're going to be so upset that you didn't recognize me.'

'I'm sorry, madam, I've never seen you.'

'You've never seen me? I was at your *bar mitzvah*!'

'There must be some mistake, lady. I'm not even Jewish.'

'No? Well, give me back my present.'

* * * * *

A postman rang the door-bell, and a woman stuck her head out of the bedroom window and yelled, 'What is it?'

'A registered parcel for Mrs Cohen.'

'Is it in gift wrapping or ordinary brown paper?'

'Ordinary brown paper.'

'Who is it from?'

'Golding and Gilman Limited.'

'From where?'

140

'Leeds.'

'What's in it?'

'I don't know. Will you come down and sign for it, please?'

'I can't.'

'Why not?'

'Because I'm not Mrs Cohen.She lives next door.'

*   *   *   *   *

Mrs Cohen was travelling on the subway and seemed much struck by the man next to her.

'Excuse my asking,' she said at length, 'but would you be Jewish?'

The man seemed a little surprised but answered graciously enough, 'No, I'm afraid not.'

Mrs Cohen did not appear to be satisfied by this, however, and nudged the man again. 'Sure you're not?'

'Quite sure,' replied the man, looking a bit rattled.

'You're sure you're not mistaken?' persisted Mrs Cohen.

Completely exasperated by now, the poor man put down his paper and said, 'Very well, madam, yes, OK, I am Jewish.'

'Funny,' said Mrs C. 'You don't *look* Jewish.'

*   *   *   *   *

Weizmann finally persuaded his elderly Russian uncle to come and live with the remainder of his family in Manhattan. Having lived all his life in a remote Siberian village, Uncle Israel was understandably much in awe of the new, modern world he came into contact with in America.

One day, while he was out exploring the city, he got lost. He dimly recalled that his nephew had told him to phone if he was ever in trouble. But Israel had never used a phone before in his life! After thinking hard for a few minutes, he decided to ask a passer-by for help.

141

A man stepped and pointed him in the direction of a public telephone box.

'But how do I operate it?' asked Israel.

'You hold the receiver in one hand, up to your ear, and dial the number with the other.'

'What!' cried Israel, in a panic. 'I can't do that — I'll have nothing to talk with!'

* * * * *

'Hey, Bennie! Bennie! What's happened to you?' shouted one man to another, running up to him in a crowded street. 'You used to be over six feet tall and look at you now. You used to have dark hair, and now it's red. And I could have sworn your eyes were blue and brown. Whatever's happened to you?'

'Are you crazy or something? My name isn't Bennie!'

'*What?*' said the other. 'Even your name you changed?'

* * * * *

Cohen decided to treat himself to a luxury cruise and was seated at the same table as a French passenger. On their first night they took their seats and ordered what they wanted to eat. '*Bon appetit*,' said the Frenchman. 'Abe Cohen,' replied Cohen politely.

At breakfast the following morning they went through the same procedure. '*Bon appetit*,' said the Frenchman. 'Abe Cohen,' replied Cohen.

But after this had happened at every meal for the next three days, Cohen had had enough and complained to a fellow passenger, 'We go through it at every meal. He tells me his name is Bon Appetit and I tell him mine is Abe Cohen. And then at the next meal, we start all over again.'

His friend laughed and explained that the French passenger was only wishing Cohen a good meal. 'That's not his name,' he said, much to Cohen's relief.

So at breakfast the next morning Cohen made a point of sitting at their table before the Frenchman arrived and when he sat down said to him, '*Bon appetit.*' The Frenchman nodded politely and said, 'Abe Cohen.'

*   *   *   *   *

Steinberg was happy. He had worked hard all his life so that he could afford a large summer house by the ocean. It was his pride and joy. And yet, it also brought problems. Every summer, when the weather was good, he would be besieged by calls from all his poor relations. And they all wanted to come and stay in his lovely house. Consequently, he never had a moment's peace as long as the sun was shining. He never knew he had so many relations!

One day, he was sitting on the patio having breakfast with a second cousin (once removed), thinking to himself that it was the same old story. However many hints he dropped, his relations would always overstay their welcome. After a while, he sighed, and said: 'I don't suppose you'll be wanting to come back and visit next year, will you? I'm sure you've got better things to do.'

'Don't do yourself down,' his relation protested. 'You're the perfect host, and this is a lovely house. What reason is there I shouldn't come again?'

'Oh, none at all,' groaned Steinberg. 'Only it's difficult to come again, if you never go away!'

*   *   *   *   *

During a visit to his cousin Hymie, Markowitz struck up a conversation one day with Goldberg, a trustee of the local synagogue. They soon got chatting about Markowitz's home town of Hankelslav.

'Do you by any chance know a man in Hankelslav called Jacob Paulofski?' asked Goldberg.

'Do I know him? Jacob Paulofski? I should say so.'

'Tell me,' continued Goldberg, 'what's he like?'

'You really want to know? Then I'll tell you. He is the most bad-tempered person in the whole of Hankelslav. His poor wife — he beats her every day. He swears at the rabbi, and ignores all the Scriptures. I know for a fact that he eats on Yom Kippur. Personally, I wouldn't trust him as far as I could throw him.'

'That's terrible. Are you absolutely sure he does all these things?' demanded Goldberg.

'Of course I'm sure,' replied Markowitz indignantly. 'Who else knows him better than I do? After all, I *am* his best friend!'

*　　　*　　　*　　　*　　　*

There's a story that used to be told about the time when Frank Sinatra, dining in a restaurant, was approached by a young man at his table. 'Mr Sinatra, my name is Bernie Rosenberg,' said the young man, 'and I've come to ask you to do me a favour.'

'What kind of favour?' asked Sinatra.

'Well, I'm here with a girl and I want to make a good impression on her. I certainly would appreciate it if you would drop by my table and say "Hi, Bernie!".'

'Sure, kid — I'll try,' said Sinatra with a smile.

A little later he got up to leave and on the way out made a point of going over to the young man and saying, 'Hi there, Bernie!'

'Don't bother me now, Frankie,' he snapped. 'Can't you see I'm busy?'

*　　　*　　　*　　　*　　　*

At his first dance, a young Jewish boy stood shyly in the corner, afraid to ask anyone to dance.

144

Friendly Relations

He spied an attractive woman sitting on her own and eventually plucked up enough courage to go over to her.

'Excuse me, miss,' he said to her hesitatingly, 'would you like to dance with me?'

'I can't dance with a child,' she said chillingly, looking at his youthful face.

'Oh, I'm very sorry,' said the boy, blushing, 'I didn't realize you were pregnant.'

*   *   *   *   *

As the guests were leaving, Mrs Goldberg turned to her hostess, and gushed: 'Thank you so much for a wonderful dinner party. Those meringues were so tasty, I had three!'

'Four, actually,' replied the hostess, 'but who's counting?'

*   *   *   *   *

Breeding is a common theme in Jewish stories, where the quality of the family stock is not an issue to be taken lightly. In his story Cousins of Convenience *Montague Glass shares a typical row about their respective forebears that takes place between the Permasenzkys, no doubt recalling countless similar confrontations that faced immigrants from eastern Europe after their arrival in the USA around the turn of the century.*

'Cousin Tilly was around this afternoon,' Mrs Permasenzky announced one evening at dinner, after her husband had taken the keener edges from his appetite with a half-pound of chopped liver and onion.

'I hope she was feeling good,' Simon Permasenzky said, 'because that woman ain't had a sick day at her own expense now for the past ten years.'

'Ain't you ashamed to talk that way about a poor woman which all her life has had nothing but one *Tzuris* after another?'

'Any woman who goes to work and marries a man which plays for a living the bull fiddle, Mommer, couldn't look forward to no winters in Florida exactly,' Permasenzky commented.

'Tilly's husband is all right, Simon,' Mrs Permasenzky said. 'All the poor feller needs is a chance.'

146

'Yow — "a chance"!' Permasenzky exclaimed. 'Who is going to give a chance to someone which all his life has had only experience playing on the bull fiddle, even if he didn't have such a ridiculous name like Harris Fishbein, Mommer.'

'And I suppose Permasenzky is a name which comes out of the mouth natural like breathing, I suppose,' Mrs Permasenzky said, bitterly, 'which many an order you slipped up on, on account when the customer tells the bookeeper to ring up Permasenzky and the bookkeeper says how do you spell it, the customer says to never mind and ring up Cohen or Goldman or some easy name like that.'

'Well if I must got to lose once in a while an order, Mommer, that's something I couldn't help, but the Permasenzkys was once a big family, Mommer, and I am the only one left,' Permasenzky said, 'and I think I told you before, Mommer, that — '

'"Before!"' Mrs Permasenzky said. 'You told it to me already a thousand times that your grandfather was the big Permasenz *Rav* from Permasenz by Posen.'

'Well, then, for the thousand-and-oneth time, Mommer,' Permansenzky retorted, 'I would also tell you that I ain't got no intentions of changing it to Perry or anything like that. Any one which has got a name like Perry is liable at any time to have somebody by the name of Perry dropping into his store and saying, "Don't you know me, Cousin Simon?" and that a highwayman *ganvered* his pocketbook on him in the subway, and couldn't I take him to his carfare home somewheres around Decatur, Illinois, or even Gervais, Oregon?'

'But if you could prove so to such people that Perry is a name you changed to only a few months since, Popper,' Mrs Permasenzky protested, 'how could such people got the nerve to touch you?'

''Senough, Mommer,' Permasenzky said. 'That I married into a bunch of distant relations with hard-luck tales couldn't be helped now. What is *vorbei* is *vorbei*, but that I should by permission of the Supreme Court, deliberately go to work and adopt a lot of Perrys which has got appendicitis without begin able to afford it, y'understand, or is going to have daughters get married on 'em and is shy two hundred fifty dollars for the wedding expenses, understand me, then all I've got to say is my peace of mind is more to me than losing a few orders on account of not having an up-to-date name.'

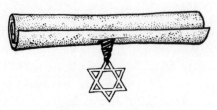

The rewards and joys of parenthood can be a very mixed blessing for the Jewish father, as this short extract from The Book of Fire *by Isaac Loebn Peretz suggests. Having catalogued a series of terrible problems with his younger daughter, who was constantly having to be bailed out of financial or legal ruin, the narrator turns to his elder daughter and the typically ill-fated destiny that awaited her husband – his son-in-law. It's little wonder that Jewish fathers took care to see who their daughters married!*

My elder daughter gave me more satisfaction. A nice respectable married woman, with five children. But my cursed luck dogged me even there.

I had married her into a rich family. His father was a big merchant in Bratkov. They lived with him on *kest* for a couple of years. Then the husband decided to start business on his own. Timber. I didn't like it. Why couldn't he have gone on studying for a few more years? But I'm used to my children not listening to me. Father and son began quarrelling. The father wanted him to buy, and he sold. The eggs always think they know better than the hens. My son-in-law didn't like having rows with his father — it was a breach of the Fifth Commandment. So he moved away to Rachov. On the Vistula. As it happens, he was doing well there. But one day there was a fire in Rachov. The police told everybody to get out of the way. A Jew who was deaf didn't move. A policeman who didn't know he was deaf decided that he was a revolutionary, deliberately flouting the orders of the state, and hit him on the head. My son-in-law couldn't stand that, and there was a row. He was trying to explain to the policeman that the man was deaf, and hadn't heard the order. But the policeman wouldn't listen, and the end of it was that he arrested both the deaf man and my son-in-law.

His rich father in Bratkov rushed at once to Rachov, and tried to buy off the police. That only made things worse. Now they said that this business must be more serious than they had thought. Because if a man was spending so much money to get the people off, they must be big men in the revolutionary movement. They sent my son-in-law to prison for six months. It ruined his business. He not only lost all his money, but he fell into debt. And he dragged his father down to ruin with him.

My daughter asked me if I could help her with some money! Would you believe it!

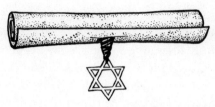

When it comes to describing Jews in the broader social dealing of the community, few writers can rival the great Yiddish author Sholom Aleichem for his penetrating and beautifully structured characterization.

Here is an extract from the opening of his book Inside Kasrilevke *which deals with his return to his small, legendary home town to visit his parents' graves. Sholom Aleichem arrives by train and having fought his way through the cabmen trying to solicit him for his fare, sits down in a horse-drawn tram (with a hole in the floor) and waits patiently until the conductor and driver decide the time is right to start off.*

His fellow passengers convey so many facets of the small-town Jew that in only a few pages the reader has a vivid impression of the people who live Inside Kasrilevke *and by extension of countless Jewish communities.*

I had no choice but to wait until the passengers straggled in. The first one to get on was a Jewish man in a tattered winter coat, the fur of which made it difficult to identify the species of animal it had once belonged to. It was too light for a fox and too red for a cat. The Jew in the ragged fur coat was followed by one without a coat, looking wretched and frozen. He sighed, glanced all around for a place and sat down in a corner by the door. After him a basket of apples staggered in,

151

and hard behind it a Jewess wrapped up in three shawls, all of them in shreds. She was visibly chilled to the bone.

'Giddap! Reb Kasriel, get a move on!' yelled Yossel the conductor to Kasriel the driver, then he let out a whistle, and the tram set in motion. But it hadn't gone more than a few paces when it came to a halt. The door of the car opened and a head appeared.

'Do you happen to know if Moishe is here?'

'Which Moishe?' Yossel the conductor asked.

'A fellow with a cap,' replied the head.

'Does he work in a hardware store?' Yossel inquired.

'That's right, in a hardware store,' the head assented.

'I know him,' the conductor rejoined, then whistled to the driver and shouted: 'Giddap! Reb Kasriel, get a move on!'

We proceeded.

'Your ticket,' the conductor called to me. 'You don't look familiar; must be from out of town. So you expect to stay here long? I can take you to a lodging house; it isn't a hotel, but it's clean and without bedbugs. And I can show you a place where you can eat cheap and you'll like the food.'

I thanked him and told him that I had acquaintances in town. He wanted to know who they were, what kind of people they were and what they did for a living. I gave him a fictitious name and got rid of him. He let go of me, stepped up to the passenger in the fur coat and told him to buy a ticket. The latter shrugged his shoulders.

'What are you talking about? Why, I haven't got a groschen to my name.'

'That's the third time this week you're travelling without a ticket,' Conductor Yossel reminded him peevishly.

'Well, what of it? Do you expect me to walk? Or maybe you want me to rob somebody, just to please you,' the fur-coated passenger replied just as peevishly.

Yossel the conductor waved his hand resignedly as he left him. He then walked up to the shivering, coatless passenger. The latter let on that he was dozing.

'See here, beg pardon, your ticket.'

The man, pretending that he had just been roused from his sleep, rubbed his hands together.

'Your ticket!' Conductor Yossel repeated.

'I heard you,' replied the passenger, coughing into his cupped hands.

'Never mind hearing me,' Conductor Yossel said to him sternly. 'Begging your pardon, fork out five kopecks and here's your ticket.'

'Shush!' the shivering passenger came back. 'What are you getting so huffy about? Just look at him — you'd think he was somebody!'

'Don't try to act smart,' Conductor Yossel retorted. 'Dish out the five kopecks.'

'Tut-tut,' the coatless one replied. 'That's a pretty steep price. I'd think you'd bring it down a bit for me.'

'I'll bring down my hard luck on your head,' Conductor Yossel rejoined.

'Better hang on to it yourself,' the shivering passenger countered. 'I've enough of my own.'

'Then I'll ask you — begging your pardon — to get off, if you don't mind.' Turning to the driver, he ordered: 'Reb Kasriel, halt.'

Kasriel the driver stopped the tram and seemed perfectly delighted about it — to say nothing of the poor nag.

'Begging your pardon — right foot first,' Conductor Yossel directed the passenger. The latter stamped his feet, rubbed his hands, and didn't budge.

'Are you waiting for a formal invitation?' Conductor Yossel asked him. 'Would you like me to grab you by the collar and chuck you out in a heap? You'd better not wait till Velvel the inspector comes around (he's attending a circumcision celebration at our treasurer's just now), or you'll catch it good and proper. Reb Kasriel, giddap,' he addressed the driver again, and the tram moved on.

'There's no justice in the world,' the woman with the

apples suddenly spoke up. 'What makes this man worse than the other one, I'd like to know. Look here, you're letting the other fellow go without a ticket, aren't you? Is it because he's wearing a fur coat and this man is in rags? Are you afraid he's going to wear a hole in your precious bench, eh? Or do you suppose they'll reward you with a golden tombstone for what you're doing?'

'Who's asking you to butt in or stick up for anybody?' Conductor Yossel wanted to know. 'How can you compare this fellow to the other man? Why, I *know* the other man; he comes of a good family. Poor fellow has come down in the world. And this chap' (pointing to the chilly one), '— who the blazes knows who he is? Just a nobody, a ragamuffin!'

'Well, supposing he is a poor man, what about it?' the apple woman argued, rising. 'Is that any reason for kicking him out? The idea of kicking out a man! Just imagine the terrible crime he's committed! Your nag is going uptown anyway, so what do you care if another man is sitting in the car? Supposing you did get five kopecks more, what then? Will that make your employer rich?'

'Look here, nobody is asking for your advice; you'd better come across with your own fare, and here's your ticket.'

'Goodness alive!' the woman started up, slapping her skirts with her hands. 'Something told me that he was going to pick on me next! Upon my word, I knew he would!'

'Well, what did you expect? Expect me to carry you for nothing?'

'What do you mean, carry me?' said the woman. 'Why, the car is carrying me; you aren't. A fellow puts on a brass button and he thinks he can boss me around. See here, Mister Conductor, I can still remember the time you worked as a helper for Leyzer Hersh, the ABC-teacher, and used to lug the little tots to school on your shoulders, with their lunch pails. So what's all this fuss about tickets-shmickets?'

Yossel didn't answer her.

'Well, what do you think of the gold mine I'm operating?'

he asked me, sitting down beside me. 'As you can see, that's what they're all like in this town. The people who have the money and are able to pay go on foot; and those that haven't got it and can't pay, ride on the tram. So how's a fellow to live and support an old mother and a widowed sister? See these boots?' — (pointing to them) — 'You can't just ignore them either. They want to eat, too.'

Suddenly there was a crash, the slamming together of two pairs of shafts, the snorting and puffing of two horses. Two coaches on the same line and going in opposite directions had run into each other. Curses flew thick:

'A plague on you! Blast you, you bloody fool! May a demon possess your father's father's father and all the generations before them to the beginning of time! ...'

'I hope those carriage shafts choke you and shove your mouth down your throat. May the demons seek out your ancestors first; you're a more worthy son.'

'What's the matter with your eyes, you hoodlum? You saw me going right, didn't you? So why couldn't you turn left?'

'And where is it written, you ugly monster, that you must go right and I must go left? Suppose it's the other way round — I go right and you go left.'

'Well, aren't you an ass? Why, that's what the two lines are for: I go this way and you go that way.'

'You're an ass yourself! Where is it written that you must go this way and that I must go that way?'

Suddenly there was a grin on the other driver's face, as he said good-naturedly:

'You know what? The devil take them, their lines and all — their cars and their whole bloody tramway! Better let's have a fag, Kasriel, old dear, if you've got one. For all I care, they can go up in a blaze along with their tramway! How's your old woman these days? Is she quieting down a bit?'

'As quiet as the river Sambatyen on weekdays. The only time she shuts up is when she's asleep. And what's new with you?'

155

'Nothing new. They're making life pretty miserable for me. I guess I'll tell them to go to the devil.'

'Don't you know what to do, you silly? Give them a piece of your mind. Tell them what's what, like me, and they'll give you anything you want.'

'May the Lord give them a grievous disease, with a triple fever for good measure! What's your boor doing? Is he going into the service soon? Or isn't it time?'

'For all I care he can go straight to hell! He's afraid of a whipping and acts dumb. . . . Have you got a match on you? Let's have a light.'

And both drivers got into a long conversation in cabmen's lingo, like the best of friends. The two conductors likewise became involved in a very chummy chat, until Velvel the inspector came along, in a jolly mood, back from the treasurer's circumcision party and raised a row:

'Confound the both of you. So you're in a devil of a mess again, eh? Lucky for you I'm feeling pretty good after our treasurer Mottel's party. I'm telling you, boys, did he throw a party! Confound him! Must be a pretty nice job handling the money. I wouldn't mind it myself. A deuce of a lot better than being an inspector and running behind the tram like a dog. Man alive, what's up with you two anyhow? Another catastrophe, eh? Another collision, well! Can't you see where you're going? What about the passengers? Well, I don't give a hang about them! It's lucky you didn't smash the cars. Anyway, boys, you've got to disentangle those trams. Look now, Kasriel old dear, rehitch the horse to the other end and drive back to the station and Reb Azriel will follow you.'

'I'd like to know why it's up to me to drive back?' Kasriel objected. 'Let Azriel rehitch his horse and let him drive back to town and I'll follow him.'

'Reb Azriel,' the inspector turned to him, 'won't you please rehitch your horse and drive back to town.'

'I should say not,' Azriel replied. 'It'll suit me quite all right if Kasriel rehitches his horse and goes back to the station. It won't hurt him a bit.'

'I'll be hanged if I do,' Kasriel shot back.

'I won't budge if it kills me,' said Azriel.

'I wish it would,' the apple woman spoke up, grabbed her basket and crawled out of the tram. 'Wasn't that a lovely ride? And that's what they want five kopecks for! If I had walked, I would have been up town ages ago. Whoever thought up that "tramby" for Kasrilevke? It's a downright disgrace!'

'The only thing to do,' I said to myself, 'is to take to my legs and march to town.'

I picked up my valise and was off on foot. A crowd of cabbies drove up behind me, whistling, shouting, and laughing:

'Well, well, so the gentleman wouldn't mix his caviar with kidney beans, eh? Just wouldn't ride with a plain coachman. Took a fancy to the "tramby", did you? You're lucky you escaped with your life. They might have flattened you to a pancake. Now you just climb into the wagon, mister, valise and all — any wagon you like. We all work hand in glove — misery in partnership. We take any affliction the Lord may send us, as long as we all get an equal share — Get a move on, boys, giddap there!'

I climbed into the covered wagon and made a triumphal entry into Kasrilevke.

*   *   *   *   *

Don't be a pal to your son. Be his father. What child needs a forty-year-old man for a friend?

Al Capp

*   *   *   *   *

157

I've Taken a Page in the Bible

The luckiest man was Adam — he had no mother-in-law.
Sholom Aleichem

*   *   *   *   *

The best security for old age — respect your children.
Sholem Asch

Laughter
Through Tears

Humour in adversity

Without a strong sense of humour the Jews would never have survived. They have managed to come through the worst possible circumstances because they have had the ability to see some glimmer of humour in the grimmest of situations. In the worst of pogroms and through the holocaust the laughter has come through the suffering, forming another powerful element in the heritage of Jewish humour.

The stories and jokes about the fate of the Jews go right back to the time of Moses, who according to at least one account was none too bright. 'When he led the Children of Israel out of Egypt,' goes one joke, 'if Moses had turned right instead of left, we'd have had the oil fields and they'd have had the oranges!' There is the logic of the Jew again.

Many Jewish stories reflect the triumph of the Jews in the face of persecution – their ability to score intellectual if not physical victories over their opponents, and this century the majority of those are centred on Nazi Germany and Soviet Russia.

President Brezhnev summoned his chief of police just before President Nixon was due to arrive and told him to have thirty synagogues built immediately.

The police chief came back and said the work had been done. 'We have Arks, Scrolls of the Law, the lot,' he said.

'But what about the rabbis,' asked Brezhnev anxiously, 'did you get thirty rabbis?'

'I'm afraid not,' said the police chief sheepishly, 'all the candidates were either not party members — or they were Jews!'

*   *   *   *   *

Hitler and Goebbels were discussing the difference between an accident and a misfortune. They could come to no conclusion, so Goebbels said: 'We will ask a Jew, he'll tell us.'

So they ordered over a passing Jew and demanded that he tell them the difference.

'I can only give you an example,' said the Jew. 'If Hitler was in a car crash, that would be an accident. If he survived, that would be a misfortune.'

*   *   *   *   *

At a meeting of the super-powers Mr Kosygin told President Nixon he had dreamed that an American flag was flying over the Capitol with Russian writing on it.

'That's strange,' replied Nixon, 'I also dreamed I saw a flag — over the Kremlin.'

'What did it say?' asked the Russian.

'I've no idea,' said Nixon. 'It was in Hebrew.'

162

During the Nazi occupation of Europe a high-ranking German officer came across a Jewish restaurant which served all his favourite Jewish dishes. He booked a table and enjoyed a meal such as he had not done for many months. But his pleasure was spoilt by a parrot that kept squawking 'a plague on Hitler' all the time. Angrily, the officer told the owner that unless the parrot was silenced he, the owner, would face a trip to the concentration camp.

The worried owner went to see his rabbi, who fortunately had a parrot of his own which he agreed to swap for the offending bird.

The Nazi officer came again the next evening and was much impressed by the way the parrot had been silenced in only twenty-four hours. Just to make sure he approached the cage and tried to encourage the bird. 'Let's hear you,' said the officer, 'a plague on Hitler, a plague on Hitler.'

'Amen,' replied the parrot.

* * * * *

In America, in the 1950s, a very rich and social-climbing society lady was fussing over the guest list for the coming-out party of her eldest daughter. She couldn't find enough eligible men and someone suggested that she contact the Westpoint Officers' Training Academy and get them to send over some 'suitable' young men.

She phoned and spoke to the General. 'So that's twelve young officers to arrive Saturday night,' she said. 'And by the way, strictly no Jews. ... You know what I mean.'

So the night arrived, and the rest of the guests made their way from the hall to the reception room and were duly announced by the toastmaster. The lady of the house was called by the butler, who explained that they were having a problem at the door. When she reached it she saw twelve black officers in uniform.

'There must be some mistake,' she stuttered.

'No, ma'am,' said the first officer. 'General Cohen never makes mistakes!'

*   *   *   *   *

A friend advised Groucho Marx confidentially that he might as well forget about applying for membership of a beach club in Santa Monica, because the committee were known to be violently anti-semitic.

'My wife isn't Jewish,' said Groucho, 'so will they let my son go into the water up to his knees?'

*   *   *   *   *

An unfortunate man so far forgot himself when talking to the nineteenth-century Anglo-Jewish philanthropist Sir Moses Montefiore one day as to make some unflattering remarks about the appearance of a Jewish lady who was standing with a group nearby. Seeing the expression on Sir Moses' face, the man hastened to apologize cravenly, 'Oh, I beg your pardon, sir. I am sorry, do forgive me. You look as though you were about to devour me!'

'Don't be ridiculous, sir, my religion forbids it,' replied Sir Moses by way of a *coup de grace*.

*   *   *   *   *

Kaiser Francis Joseph of Austria appointed Rabbi Simon Sofer to a seat in parliament, even though Jews had no citizens' rights in the country at that time.

On his first day the rabbi entered parliament, and headed for a seat on the left of the house — where the socialists normally sat.

When the session was over the speaker came up and asked Rabbi Sofer why he had chosen to sit on the left.

'Jews have no rights!' was the prompt reply.

164

A Russian policeman saw a Jew walking along a street in Moscow at a period when Jews were not supposed to visit the city.

'What are you doing here?' the policeman thundered. 'Where is your passport?'

The Jew handed him the document which showed he had been born in Moscow. Frustrated by this attempt to find fault, the policeman pointed to the cap the Jew had forgotten to take off during the questioning. 'And what about the hat?' he snapped.

'Don't worry,' said the Jew, 'that comes from Moscow too!'

*   *   *   *   *

The potato crop in Russia had failed again because of drought. As part of a campaign to get more people producing potatoes, a government official visited a Jewish peasant farmer and asked him how his crop was faring.

'If I were to place all my potatoes on top of each other in one great heap they would reach the heavenly throne,' said the peasant.

At this the official became annoyed. 'Don't be stupid,' he said, 'this is a communist country and everyone knows there is no Almighty and no heavenly throne.'

'That's exactly what I mean,' said the Jew, 'and there are no potatoes either.'

*   *   *   *   *

One day an elderly Jewish man sat on a park bench in Moscow Central Park, reading a Hebrew book. He was quite open about it; his head was covered and he swayed as he read. Suddenly a KGB man appeared from nowhere and, obviously furious with this blatant anti-Russian expression, he shouted at the man.

'Old man, what are you doing?'

165

'I'm reading a Hebrew book,' came the reply.

The KGB man was enraged. 'Why are you reading a book in Hebrew?' he asked. 'You're far too old for us to let you settle in Israel. . . . Why do you bother?'

'You forget,' said the old man. 'They speak Hebrew in Heaven.'

The KGB man was furious. 'Heaven! What makes you think you'll go to Heaven? Maybe you'll go to Hell.'

'In that case,' smiled the old man, 'Russian I already know.'

*   *   *   *   *

An old rabbi found himself sharing a railway carriage with a Russian officer as they travelled from Moscow to Irkutsk. Neither spoke for the first hundred miles, then the Russian suddenly grabbed the rabbi and demanded: 'Why are you Jews so clever? Why do you rule the world?'

'Clever — I don't know,' said the Jew. 'I expect it's because we eat fish.'

Nothing further was said for another hundred miles. Then the rabbi unwrapped the parcel he was carrying, took out a herring and ate it.

'How many have you got left?' the Russian asked.

'Twelve.'

'I'll buy them. How much do you want?'

'Twenty roubles.'

The Russian paid his money and began to eat his first fish. He had only taken a couple of bites when he suddenly grabbed the rabbi for a second time saying: 'Wait a minute — I gave you twenty roubles for these. In Moscow they only cost a few kopecks.'

'There, you see,' said the rabbi, 'it's starting to work already.'

*   *   *   *   *

During a bad harvest in the Soviet Union, when food was scarce, a government inspector called on farms to see how matters could be improved.

Eventually he visited a Jewish farmer, and asked him how he fed his chickens.

'With stale bread crusts,' replied the farmer.

'In that case you are fined twenty-five roubles,' said the inspector, 'because the bread could have been used to feed people.'

He came to a second Jewish farmer and asked him also how he kept his chickens alive.

'I feed them carrot tops,' replied the farmer.

'They could have been used to make a soup,' said the inspector. 'You're fined twenty-five roubles.'

The inspector set off to see a third Jewish farmer, but the first two Jews managed to smuggle a note to their friend to warn him of the visit.

The inspector arrived and asked the third Jewish farmer the same question: 'How do you feed your chickens?'

'I don't, sir,' replied the Jew. 'I give them 10 kopecks each and tell them to buy their own dinner!'

*   *   *   *   *

A Jew was sitting peaceably on a train one afternoon, when he was spotted by two members of the Hitler Youth. Deciding to annoy him, they took up positions on the seats on either side of him.

'So, Jew,' began the first youth contemptuously, 'can you help my friend and me? We were wondering if you were a complete imbecile or just a nasty piece of work?'

The Jew contemplated the question for a few moments while the two youths laughed inanely, then answered calmly: 'It's a difficult question, but I think I can safely say that I am somewhere between the two.'

167

I've Taken a Page in the Bible

One of the many bizarre facts about Adolf Hitler is that he was susceptible to superstition and the supernatural. The story goes that he went one day to consult a famous astrologer and asked whether he could predict the day on which he, Adolf Hitler, would die.

The astrologer consulted his cards and after a slight hesitation said, 'You will die on a Jewish holiday.'

This was a bit hard for the dictator to take, of course, and he demanded sharply, 'Which Jewish holiday?'

The astrologer shrugged his shoulders and said, 'I can't say which one.'

'You must,' cried Hitler.

'I can't,' repeated the astrologer, 'any day you die will be a Jewish holiday.'

*　　*　　*　　*　　*

A Jewish woman, living in Berlin when the Nazis were in power, went to the post office to complain. 'The stamps don't stick on to the envelopes properly,' she told the clerk.

'But you have to spit on them,' said the clerk.

'Oh I do,' said the woman, 'but they still don't stick.'

'Which side do you spit on?' asked the clerk.

'Well, on the pictures, of course!' said the woman.

*　　*　　*　　*　　*

A Jew named Rosenthal was involved in a court case against a German named Muller during the days of Hitler. At that time it was nearly impossible for Jews to win cases against non-Jews. On this occasion the judge was a very strict man, and any attempt to bribe him always resulted in the other side winning the dispute. While he was waiting for the decision Rosenthal was boasting to a friend that he was bound to win, because he had sent the judge a very fine present.

'Oh, no,' said the friend, 'now you have no hope — this judge is very strict about not taking bribes.'

'I know,' said Rosenthal, 'so I put in a card reading "With compliments of Mr Muller"!'

*   *   *   *   *

A Nazi judge addressed a Jew who had applied for his name to be changed. 'This is typical of you Jews,' he said. 'You try to fool gentiles by adopting our names. Well it won't work this time,' the judge went on, 'your name is Mayer and Mayer it will remain!'

'Your honour,' replied the Jew quietly. 'It's my first name I want to change — from Adolf to Abraham.'

*   *   *   *   *

A Jew in Hitler's Germany was discovered reading an anti-semitic newspaper. His friend was incredulous. 'How on earth can you bring yourself to look at such a disgusting publication?'

The first Jew explained. 'The Jewish papers make me very sad — they are always saying, "Jews kicked out of the capital", "Jews banned from public places", and the like. 'But when I read the anti-semitic papers, they say, "Jews control the world", and "World finance is in Jewish hands", and it makes me very proud!'

*   *   *   *   *

Hitler's attempts to conquer Britain had failed, partly because of problems in getting so many men across the English Channel. Feeling thwarted, he told a medium to conjure up the spirit of Moses for him.

'Can I ask a question?' Hitler asked the spirit.

'Yes,' said Moses. 'What is it?'

'How did you make the Red Sea divide?' asked Hitler.
'It was easy,' said Moses, 'I used my wooden rod.'
'Wonderful!' said Hitler.'Where it it now?'
'At the British Museum in London,' said Moses.

*   *   *   *   *

The German Minister of Propaganda, Goebbels, was always on the lookout for new ways to promote the Nazi cause. One day he visited a high school in the days before Jewish pupils were kicked out.

Goebbels addressed the students at a gathering in the school hall. 'Any student who can come up with a good slogan for our propaganda work will get a prize,' he said.

At the back of the hall a student got up and suggested 'Germany Above All'. 'Good,' said the minister, 'any more?'

Near the front a small student got up and said, 'We shall live for ever!'

Goebbels was delighted. 'Excellent, you win the prize. What's your name?'

'Isaac Goldberg,' answered the student.

*   *   *   *   *

Sometimes it isn't possible to get the better of adversaries, but even then the Jews have been able to laugh in the face of persecution, extracting humour from predicaments that would be truly unbearable without the leavening effect of laughter.

Whether they are faced with conscious victimization or unconscious – but no less damning – antisemitisim, Jews can invariably find something funny in the situation. There are stories of seemingly futile individual protests; ones that contrast the lot of the Jew with the freedom enjoyed by the gentile; and others that take the Jew's peculiar powers of reasoning and apply them to the hostile world of persecution.

My dear Lisl,
    Since Hitler took over Czechoslovakia, life is wonderful. We are all very happy and everything is fine.

Love from Maria

PS Uncle Rudla, who did not agree, was buried yesterday.

*   *   *   *   *

The war had ended and in the Russian sector of East Berlin the authorities were busy renaming all the streets. An old Jew who had managed to survive in the city got on a tram one day in the eastern sector and asked the conductor, 'Would you please let me off at Stissenstrasse?'

'Certainly, comrade. Sit down... Stissenstrasse, comrade?'

'Yes, please,' said the old Jew.

The tram stopped. 'Stalinstrasse... formerly Hitlerstrasse,' said the conductor. The little Jew got up. 'No, not yet, comrade,' the conductor told him. 'I'll let you know when we get to your stop.'

At the second stop the conductor shouted, 'Leninstrasse... formerly Goeringstrasse.' Again the little Jew got up. 'No, not yet, comrade,' said the conductor. 'I'll tell you when.'

The tram stopped a third time. 'Karl Marx Platz... formerly Goebbels Platz,' announced the conductor, and said to the little Jew, 'No, not yet, sit down. I'll tell you when, comrade... formerly Jew bastard.'

*   *   *   *   *

A Jewish worker was chosen as a delegate to a Communist convention in Leningrad. He arrived at the conference hall and for the first time in his life he saw a microphone. 'What on earth is that?' the Jew asked his neighbour.

'It's called a microphone,' said the delegate. 'When you talk into it everyone can hear what you say.'

'I would love to say one word into it,' said the Jew. His neighbour agreed to arrange it and during a break the Russian delegate went over to the chairman and said, 'There's a delegate here who would like to say a word over the microphone.' The chairman said this was in order and said he would call for the man.

So the Jew's name was announced. He got up, walked to the platform, grabbed the microphone with both hands, cleared his throat and shouted, 'Help!'

Two young Jews could not agree about life in the Soviet Union. Finally one of them said, 'Next year I'm going to Russia, and find out for myself. I will write to you and say what things are like. If conditions are OK, I'll use blue ink, if bad I'll write in green ink.'

The other agreed to this and next year he received a glowing letter from his friend in Russia, which stated how wonderful things were.

'The shops are full of everything, the people dress well, and the morale is very good,' said the letter. 'You can get everything you need here, except for one small thing — green ink!'.

* * * * *

An American Jew went to Moscow and met a leading Russian official. It was when Nixon had just been elected President of the US and they soon got around to discussing the merits of dictatorship and democracy.

The American said, 'In the States I could say Nixon was a useless idiot and nothing would happen to me.'

'You could say the same thing here and nothing would happen to you either!' said the Russian.

* * * * *

An Israeli journalist was interviewing a recent immigrant from the Soviet Union. 'How was your flat?' asked the reporter.

'I had no complaint.'

'Well, how was your job then?'

'I had no complaint,' came the reply again.

'Then why did you come here?' asked the exasperated reporter.

'Because here I *can* complain,' said the immigrant.

I've Taken a Page in the Bible

A Jewish peasant living in Russia decided to make a trip to Moscow.

When in the capital he visited the tomb of Lenin. Flowers and wreaths hung lavishly all around the walls of the mausoleum. The astonished Jew approached a guard and asked him how much all the decorations cost. 'Fifteen thousand roubles,' was the reply.

'Good God!' said the Jew, 'We could have buried the entire politbureau for that amount!'

He was arrested and sentenced to one year's hard labour and two years' parole. He worked his time and left, thinking, 'You can't play games with these people — I'll become a Communist.' So he got two photos, one of Stalin, the other of Lenin, and hung them on his wall.

The Jew's probation officer called, saw the photos and yelled, 'Remove the bastard!'

'Which one?' asked the Jew, for which he was arrested, and sentenced to three years' hard labour and another three years' probation.

Eventually he finished his sentence, and vowed, 'You can't play games with these people, I'll become a party member.' So he did, attending all the meetings and reading as many books as he could find on the subject.

One day he was forced to miss a meeting through illness. Later, on the street, he met a comrade, who asked him why he hadn't come to the last meeting.

'What, the *last* meeting, was it?' said the Jew. 'If I had known it was the last meeting I would have come even if I was at death's door!'

He was sent to a camp in Siberia for ten years.

*   *   *   *   *

While working for the US Embassy in Moscow a wealthy American Jew went to the bank to cash a cheque. To his

174

amazement he saw the cashier sitting casually at a desk in the lobby, with a stack of banknotes in front of him.

The Jew went over to him. 'Do you realize,' he said, 'that in the States a cashier sits in a locked cage with the money in a safe?'

'Ah, that's because with you Americans money is important,' said the cashier, 'So you keep it locked up. With us Russians, on the other hand, people are important — so we keep *them* locked up!'

*   *   *   *   *

While in Leningrad a Jewish visitor developed toothache, and in great pain he went to a dentist, who was also Jewish. The dentist looked inside the Jew's mouth and said it would cost £200 to have the tooth removed.

'£200 to have my tooth pulled out?' screamed the Jew. 'How can it possibly cost that much?'

'Well, I'm afraid I shall have to take it out through the jaw,' said the dentist.

'Through the jaw?' queried the patient. 'Why not through the mouth?'

'Because,' said the dentist, 'no one in Russia is allowed to *open* his mouth!'

*   *   *   *   *

Golda Meir lay dying. In hospital she received many visitors, but was flabbergasted to see ex-President Brezhnev walk through the door.

'Golda,' he said. 'You are going to die, and although we've been enemies for a long, long time, I just had to come and say my last goodbyes to you.'

'Brezhnev, thank you for coming. You and I have battled for many years. Now I am about to die, I wish you to do me a favour. Brezhnev, open the gates of Russia for one day, just

175

one day, and let all those who wish to enter the country enter, and all those who wish to leave, leave.'

Brezhnev laughed and winked at Golda. 'I understand, Golda, you want us to be alone there together!'

*   *   *   *   *

Mrs Mandelbaum sent her husband a telegram from Moscow which read, 'SAYS TO OPERATE OPERATE'.

Mr Mandelbaum cabled back: 'SAYS TO OPERATE OPERATE'.

Made suspicious by such cryptic messages, the KGB paid a call on Mr Mandelbaum and said, 'All right, Mandelbaum, we know you're using code. What are you and that wife of yours plotting?'

'Plotting? Code?' repeated Mr Mandelbaum.

'Yes, we're no fools, we have your telegrams.'

'Oh, those! Let me explain,' cried Mr Mandelbaum. 'You see, my wife has a sick stomach and she's been to the doctors in Moscow. She sends me: 'SAYS TO OPERATE. OPERATE?' I send her: 'SAYS TO OPERATE? OPERATE!'

*   *   *   *   *

A Jewish schoolboy called Jacob complained to his mother that whenever a ball was thrown to him during games at school the others would shout, 'Catch it, Jew,' instead of using his name.

His mother, a formidable lady, was naturally distressed at this news and called upon the games master at his home to tell him of what was happening. Having listened to her complaint he agreed to do something about it.

At the next games lesson the boys were playing happily when someone threw a ball to Jacob. 'Catch it, Jew,' said the boy. At this the games master blew his whistle and rushed over to the offending pupil.

'How dare you!' he shouted at the boy. 'You must never say that again — how would you like to be called a Jew?'

*   *   *   *   *

A train pulled out of a station and, a moment later, a black man entered a compartment in which a Jew was already seated. To the Jew's amazement, the black began to read a Yiddish newspaper. After a moment the Jew could not restrain himself and leaning forward asked, 'Being black isn't enough for you?'

*   *   *   *   *

A elderly Christian woman, noted for her dislike of Jews, was deciding where to go on holiday. She went to the travel agent and said: 'I want to go on holiday this year — I don't care where as long as it is warm and there are no Jews.'

'How about Hell?' replied the Jewish counter clerk.

*   *   *   *   *

177

Jews can even find humour in the pathos of their predicament. There are stories that verge on the tragic — black humour if you like — that reflect the extraordinary powers of endurance that Jews have cultivated. There can be an almost wistful memory of the persecutors, just as former captives can sometimes form an attachment to their captors. This is a bitter-sweet humour reflecting both the resignation and the resilience of the Jew.

Having survived the concentration camp but having lost all his family, a Jewish refugee was asked where he would like to be resettled. He declared, 'In Australia.'

'But that's so far away,' the official exclaimed.

'From where?' the Jew asked.

*　　*　　*　　*　　*

An officer on a British boat went to a Jewish refugee's cabin and was amazed to see a framed photograph of Hitler standing on a shelf. 'How can you bear to have that man's picture with you?' he asked the Jew.

'It was very hard to leave my home,' was the reply, 'so I keep that to cure any homesickness.'

*　　*　　*　　*　　*

178

One day a Cossack was taking part in a pogrom in a small Russian *shteitel*. He rode astride his horse, swinging his sword left and right, killing all those in his path. Then he came across a Jew, whom he grabbed by the ears and held dangling next to his steed.

'The whole country is going to the dogs and it's all the fault of the Jews!' the Cossack shouted.

'And the bicycle-makers,' said the Jew.

The Russian looked at him in amazement. 'The bicycle-makers? Why the bicycle-makers?'

The Jew shrugged his shoulders. 'Why the Jews?'

*   *   *   *   *

Two Jews are up against the wall and the captain of the firing squad asks if they have any last requests. The first Jew asks for a cigarette; his friend, as a last gesture, spits in the captain's face.

'Please, Benny,' says the first, 'Don't make trouble.'

*   *   *   *   *

A couple of poor Jews who hadn't seen each other for several years met by chance on a street in Warsaw. 'How are you, my friend? How do you like it in Warsaw?' one asked the other.

'I'm getting along all right, but I'd have been better off if I hadn't been ill for two months. That cost me two hundred roubles.'

'Two hundred roubles!' whistled his friend. 'That's too bad. I tell you, as sure as I'm living, back home in Lithuania a man could be ill for two years for that much money.'

*   *   *   *   *

An American Jewish tourist in Israel was surprised and distressed by the sight of an old man praying fervently with

179

tears pouring down his face. When the American asked the old man what the matter was, he was even more surprised to be told, 'I want to be with my people.'

'But surely you are? You are in Israel!'

'No, no,' wailed the old man. 'I mean my people in Miami!'

*　　*　　*　　*　　*

It was during the dark days of the First World War and Warsaw seemed likely to fall to the German army. Concerned about the situation, Czar Nicholas went disguised as a civilian to discover the morale of his troops. 'What's your view about Warsaw's fate?' he asked a Polish soldier.

'We shall fight them till the bitter end,' came the reply. Then the Czar asked an Englishman for his opinion, who replied, 'We shall fight to the last Pole.' Finally, the Czar approached a Jewish soldier and asked again, 'What's your view about Warsaw's fate?'

'If I were the Czar,' said the Jew, 'I would transfer it to my wife's name.'

*　　*　　*　　*　　*

Perhaps the greatest single triumph in the face of adversity is the creation of the state of Israel, which features in many modern Jewish stories and reveals all the dominant themes picked up in others in this collection.

Just after the creation of Israel a young volunteer named Cohen decided to do his bit for his new country. So he tried to join the Army, but was told to come back later as they had no uniforms at the moment.

Next he went to the Navy, where immediately he was asked if he could swim. 'Oh no!' said Cohen. 'Don't tell me you've got no boats!'

*   *   *   *   *

During his time as Deputy Prime Minister of Israel, Abba Eban was asked by an interviewer, 'Do you face special problems in Israel as a result of such a large proportion of your population being so young?'

'Fortunately,' said Eban with a smile, 'this is a problem that will be resolved with the passing of time.'

*   *   *   *   *

I've Taken a Page in the Bible

President Truman invited Israel's first president, Chaim Weitzman, for a meeting to discuss the new State's future.

'Tell me,' said Truman, 'what does your country need?'

'Everything that begins with the letter A,' replied Dr Weitzman. 'A billion dollars, a million Jews, a million more factories...'

* * * * *

During a period of uneasy peace on the Israeli-Jordanian border, two border-guards were patrolling with guard dogs on either side of the line. The Jordanian guard had a savage rotweiler and the Israeli guard had a curious-looking dachshund, though a good bit bigger than the normal size for the breed.

'We are stupid, you know,' said the Jordanian guard as they passed on one occasion. 'We fight over territory, sacrificing thousands of men. You want five yards of our territory, I want five yards of your territory, why don't we let our dogs do the fighting instead?'

To his surprise the Israeli guard agreed and, certain he was in for an easy win, the Jordanian unleashed his dog. Before it could move, though, the large dachshund lunged at its throat and killed it with a single bite.

'My God, what sort of dog is that?' asked the Jordanian in amazement.

'I can't tell you,' said the Israeli, 'but before we had its nose taken in it was a crocodile.'

* * * * *

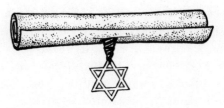

Woody Allen requires no introduction from me. His wit and perception are famous to millions of fans of his films and articles. No Kaddish for Weinstein *comes from the collection of his writing* Without Feathers, *and portrays in a hilariously surreal way the frustrations a Jew can feel in a hostile world. (The* kaddish *is one of the most solemn and oldest Jewish prayers; the one also said by mourners over the grave of a deceased relative on every anniversary of the death.)*

Weinstein lay under the covers, staring at the ceiling in a depressed torpor. Outside sheets of humid air rose from the pavement in stifling waves. The sound of traffic was deafening at this hour, and in addition to all this his bed was on fire. Look at me, he thought. Fifty years old. Half a century. Next year, I will be fifty-one. Then fifty-two. Using this same reasoning, he could figure out his age as much as five years in the future. So little time left, he thought, and so much to accomplish. For one thing, he wanted to learn to drive a car. Adelman, his friend who used to play dreidel with him on Rush Street, had studied driving and had already driven many places by himself. Weinstein had made a few attempts to steer his father's Chevy but kept winding up on the sidewalk.

He had been a precocious child. An intellectual. At twelve, he had translated the poems of T. S. Eliot into English, after some vandals had broken into the library and translated them into French. And as if his high IQ did not isolate him enough, he suffered untold injustices and persecutions because of his religion, mostly from his parents. True, the old man was a member of the synagogue, and his mother, too, but they could never accept the fact that their son was Jewish. 'How did it happen?' his father asked, bewildered. My face looks Semitic, Weinstein thought every morning as he shaved. He had been mistaken several times for Robert Redford, but on each occasion it was by a blind person. Then there was Feinglass, his other boyhood friend: A Phi Beta Kappa. A labor spy, ratting on the workers. Then a convert to Marxism. A Communist agitator. Betrayed by the Party, he went to Hollywood and became the offscreen voice of a famous cartoon mouse. Ironic.

Weinstein had toyed with the Communists, too. To impress a girl at Rutgers, he had moved to Moscow and joined the Red Army. When he called her for a second date, she was pinned to someone else. Still, his rank of sergeant in the Russian infantry would hurt him later when he needed a security clearance in order to get the free appetizer with his dinner at Longchamps. Also, while at school he had organized some laboratory mice and led them in a strike over work conditions. Actually, it was not so much the politics as the poetry of Marxist theory that got him. He was positive that collectivization could work if everyone would learn the lyrics to 'Rag Mop'. 'The withering away of the state' was a phrase that had stayed with him, ever since his uncle's nose had withered away in Saks Fifth Avenue one day. What, he wondered, can be learned about the true essence of social revolution? Only that it should never be attempted after eating Mexican food.

The depression shattered Weinstein's Uncle Meyer, who kept his fortune under his mattress. When the market crashed, the government called in all mattresses, and Meyer became a pauper overnight. All that was left for him was to jump out the window, but he lacked the nerve and sat on a window sill of the Flatiron Building from 1930 to 1937.

'These kids with their pot and their sex,' Uncle Meyer was fond of saying. 'Do they know what it is to sit on a window sill for seven years? There you see life! Of course, everybody looks like ants. But each year Tessie — may she rest in peace — made the Seder right out there on the ledge. The family gathered round for Passover. Oy, nephew! What's the world coming to when they have a bomb that can kill more people than one look at Max Rifkin's daughter?'

Weinstein's so-called friends had all knuckled under to the House Un-American Activities Committee. Blotnick was turned in by his own mother. Sharpstein was turned in by his answering service. Weinstein had been called by the committee and admitted he had given money to the Russian War Relief, and then added, 'Oh, yes, I bought Stalin a dining-room set.' He refused to name names but said if the committee insisted he would give the heights of the people he had met at meetings. In the end he panicked, and instead of taking the Fifth Amendment, took the Third, which enabled him to buy beer in Philadelphia on Sunday.

Weinstein finished shaving and got into the shower. He lathered himself, while steaming water splashed down his bulky back. He thought, 'Here I am at some fixed point in time and space, taking a shower. I, Isaac Weinstein. One of God's creatures.' And then, stepping on the soap, he slid across the floor and rammed his head into the towel rack. It had been a bad week. The previous day, he had got a bad haircut and was still not over the anxiety it caused him. At first the barber had snipped judiciously, but soon Weinstein realized he had gone too far. 'Put some back!' he screamed unreasonably.

'I can't,' the barber said. 'It won't stick.'

185

'Well, then give it to me, Dominic! I want to take it with me!'

'Once it's on the floor of the shop it's mine, Mr Weinstein.'

'Like hell! I want my hair!'

He blustered and raged, and finally felt guilty and left. Goyim, he thought. One way or another, they get you.

Now he emerged from the hotel and walked up Eighth Avenue. Two men were mugging an elderly lady. My God, thought Weinstein, time was when one person could handle that job. Some city. Chaos everyplace. Kant was right: The mind imposes order. It also tells you how much to tip. What a wonderful thing, to be conscious! I wonder what the people in New Jersey do.

He was on his way to see Harriet about the alimony payments. He still loved Harriet, even though while they were married she had systematically attempted to commit adultery with all the *R*s in the Manhattan telephone directory. He forgave her. But he should have suspected something when his best friend and Harriet took a house in Maine together for three years, without telling him where they were. He didn't *want* to see it — that was it. His sex life with Harriet had stopped early. He slept with her once on the night they first met, once on the evening of the first moon landing, and once to test if his back was all right after a slipped disc. 'It's no damn good with you, Harriet,' he used to complain. 'You're too pure. Every time I have an urge for you I sublimate it by planting a tree in Israel. You remind me of my mother.' (Molly Weinstein, may she rest in peace, who slaved for him and made the best stuffed derma in Chicago — a secret recipe until everyone realized she was putting in hashish.)

For lovemaking, Weinstein needed someone quite opposite. Like LuAnne, who made sex an art. The only trouble was she couldn't count to twenty without taking her shoes off. He once tried giving her a book on existentialism, but she ate it. Sexually, Weinstein had always felt inadequate. For one thing, he felt short. He was five-four in his stockinged feet, although in someone else's stockinged feet he could be as tall as five-six. Dr Klein, his analyst, got him to see that jumping in front of a moving train was more hostile than self-destructive but in either case would ruin the crease in his pants. Klein was his third analyst. His first was a Jungian, who suggested they try a Ouija board. Before that, he attended 'group', but when it came time for him to speak he got dizzy and could only recite the names of all the planets. His problem was women, and he knew it. He was impotent with any woman who finished college with higher than a B-minus average. He felt at home with graduates of typing school, although if the woman did over sixty words a minute he panicked and could not perform.

Weinstein rang the bell to Harriet's apartment, and suddenly she was standing before him. Swelling to maculate giraffe, as usual, thought Weinstein. It was a private joke that neither of them understood.

'Hello, Harriet,' he said.

'Oh, Ike,' she said. 'You needn't be so damn self-righteous.'

She was right. What a tactless thing to have said. He hated himself for it.

'How are the kids, Harriet?'

'We never had any kids, Ike.'

'That's why I thought four hundred dollars a week was a lot for child support.'

She bit her lip, Weinstein bit his lip. Then he bit her lip. 'Harriet,' he said, 'I ... I'm broke. Egg futures are down.'

'I see. And can't you get help from your *shiksa*?'

'To you, any girl who's not Jewish is a *shiksa*.'

'Can we forget it?' Her voice was choked with recrimination. Weistein had a sudden urge to kiss her, or if not her, somebody.

'Harriet, where did we go wrong?'

'We never faced reality.'

187

'It wasn't my fault. You said it was north.'

'Reality *is* north, Ike.'

'No, Harriet. Empty dreams are north. Reality is west. False hopes are east, and I think Louisiana is south.'

She still had the power to arouse him. He reached out for her, but she moved away and his hand came to rest in some sour cream.

'Is that why you slept with your analyst?' he finally blurted out. His face was knotted with rage. He felt like fainting but couldn't remember the proper way to fall.

'That was therapy,' she said coldly. 'According to Freud, sex is the royal road to the unconscious.'

'Freud said *dreams* are the road to the unconscious.'

'Sex, dreams — you're going to nit-pick?'

'Goodbye, Harriet.'

It was no use. *Rien à dire, rien à faire.* Weinstein left and walked over to Union Square. Suddenly hot tears burst forth, as if from a broken dam. Hot, salty tears pent up for ages rushed in an unabashed wave of emotion. The problem was, they were coming out of his ears. Look at this, he thought; I can't even cry properly. He dabbed his ear with Kleenex and went home.

*   *   *   *   *

The outlook of the ghetto divided the Universe into two: this world for the gentiles, the hereafter for the Jews.

David Ben-Gurion

*   *   *   *   *

In Israel in order to be a realist, you must believe in miracles.

David Ben-Gurion

*   *   *   *   *

Conversations and negotiations with Arabs are not unlike chasing a mirage in the desert: full of promise and good to look at, but likely to lead to death by thirst.

Chaim Weizmann

*   *   *   *   *

The world is divided into two groups of nations — those that want to expel the Jews and those that do not want to receive them.

Chaim Weizmann

*   *   *   *   *

If my theory of relativity is proven successful, Germany will claim me as a German and France will declare that I am a citizen of the world. If my theory should prove to be untrue, then France will say that I am a German, and Germany will say that I am a Jew.

Albert Einstein

*   *   *   *   *

Put three Zionists in a room, and they'll form four political parties.

Levi Eshkol

*   *   *   *   *

If there were no Jews they would have to be invented for the use of politicians — they are indispensable, the antithesis of a panacea; guaranteed to cause all evils.

Israel Zangwill

*   *   *   *   *

189

A Russian peasant once pronounced this mathematical theory: 'Four and four make eight, with this I can agree; some say that five and three also make eight — but that's a Jewish trick.'

Vladimir Jabotinsky

*   *   *   *   *

When people talk about a wealthy man of my creed they call him an Israelite; but if he is poor, they call him a Jew.

Heinrich Heine

*   *   *   *   *

Logical
Illogicality

The mainstay of the Jew

If there can be said to be one common element linking all Jewish humour, it has to be the Jew's wonderfully developed sense of the illogical. In a world that has such a poor opinion of Jews it is illogical, after all, to be a Jew.

Whether you take the wisdom of the people of Chelm, the Jewish mother, the reasoning applied to so much business, or the facility to laugh at thousands of years of hardship, the illogical approach to life is as deeply rooted in the Jew as his sense of humour.

In this concluding section I have collected stories that I feel point up this quality. They deal with doctors and health, and matters of life and death; life in the army; art appreciation and the law – fields of activity which, interestingly, Jews have shone in.

Old Mr Bloom was waiting to see the young doctor who had recently taken up practice in his town. He was the last patient the doctor had to see in what had been a particularly long and hard day.

'OK, Mr Bloom,' called the doctor, a little offhand. 'What's your problem?'

'What's my problem?' exclaimed the old man. 'Hmph! You study medicine for ten years, and you want me to make the diagnosis!'

*   *   *   *   *

An old Jewish tailor went to see the doctor.

'You only have one option,' said the doctor after examining him. 'You give up smoking, or your eyesight will go.'

The old tailor shrugged his shoulders.

'Doctor,' he said. 'I've lived on this earth for eighty-five years. Tell me, how much is there left to see?'

*   *   *   *   *

Soloman had been suffering for some time with a bad heart, tuberculosis, and a slipped disc. He had been confined to bed for weeks on end. Now he was on the road to recovery and a young doctor came to give him a check-up. After giving him a thorough examination, he gave his opinion. His tone of hearty optimism seemed rather out of place, considering what Soloman had been through the last couple of months.

'You're looking good, Sol,' he beamed. 'Heart's great!

Lungs are puffing away like troopers! You've still got a slipped disc, but that doesn't worry me.'

'Doctor,' said Solomon with venom, 'if you had a slipped disc, believe me, it wouldn't worry me either!'

*   *   *   *   *

There were four practising physicians serving a small community of only two hundred in the Baltic state of Lithuania. None of them had any formal training, but while in the army they had been in the Sanitary Division. Here, by listening to doctors discussing cases, they managed to pick up some knowledge of medical treatment.

One day a visitor to the community was puzzled by the number of physicians in such a small town, and asked the local rabbi why they were all needed.

The rabbi explained it to him. 'They are all experts on stomach ache, he said. 'The first physician diagnoses the case as constipation. The second then prescribes the medicine, an enema. The third knows what ingredients go into the enema. And the fourth knows the place where the pipe should be inserted!'

*   *   *   *   *

The veteran American comedian Harry Hershfield used to tell the story of an elderly Jew, a commuter on the New York subway all his life, who was struck down with a heart-attack one morning while waiting for his train.

'My friend,' said the rabbi who was summoned to his side, 'it is time to make your peace with God. Your prayers may determine whether you go to Heaven or to Hell.'

'Rabbi, I don't really care which place I'm going,' answered the dying man, 'just as long as I don't have to change in the Bronx.'

195

I've Taken a Page in the Bible

Sammy Feldman had been going to the same restaurant for many years. He always ate the same meal, never causing any trouble, never making any fuss.

Then, one evening, after the waiter had brought him his usual bowl of soup to start, he noticed something was wrong.

'Waiter, will you taste this soup?' said Sammy.

'Is there anything wrong, sir?' asked the waiter, a little worried.

'Just taste it,' requested Sammy.

'Look, sir,' continued the waiter, 'if there's anything wrong, I'll go and get you another bowl immediately.'

'Please, just taste it.'

'I don't want to argue about it, sir, believe me. I know you're not the sort of person to complain without a good reason. Let me change it.'

'For God's sake, man,' cried Sammy, his face reddening. 'Just taste the goddamn soup!'

The waiter decided it was no use arguing with Sammy. 'As you wish, sir.' Then he realized that something was missing. 'Where's your spoon?'

'Ah-*hah*!' shouted Sammy triumphantly.

*　　*　　*　　*　　*

Some well-known Jewish comedians were standing around at a party swapping jokes. As usual, each was trying to outdo the other, by telling a favourite joke. After an hour or so, another fellow comedian walked through the door, and was beckoned over to the group.

'Hey, Barney, how's tricks?' asked one of their number, and then noticed that Barney wasn't exactly smiling. 'What's the matter?'

'It's been a terrible day, fellers,' said Barney. 'This morning my wife and kids packed their bags and left. Then on the way to the supermarket, I crashed my brand-new car, and got booked by the police. When I got home, I realized that I'd left the bath running. The whole flat was flooded, and the guy downstairs too, who's suing. What a day!'

The minute Barney had finished, the person next to him cut in: 'You think *that's* funny? Wait till you hear this one!'

*   *   *   *   *

Jacob Obermeister had been charged with theft after being caught stealing some jewellery from Wringley's. As far as the police were concerned, it was an open and shut case. Soon afterwards, Jacob was brought to trial.

'How do you plead?' asked the judge.

'Excuse me, your honour,' began Jacob. 'Before I enter a plea, may I request that the court appoint me a lawyer.'

'Of course, you can have a lawyer. However, since you admit that you were caught red-handed, I fail to see what a lawyer could possibly say in your defence.'

'I couldn't agree with you more, your honour, in fact that's just what I mean,' replied Jacob. 'You see, I too am curious to hear what a lawyer could possibly say!'

*   *   *   *   *

Albert Einstein was an enthusiastic amateur violinist and during his time at Princeton he was once visited by Jascha Heifetz, Artur Rubinstein and Gregor Piatigorsky, who during the course of their stay invited him to join them in a little chamber music.

They were a few minutes into a delicate quartet when Rubinstein suddenly brought the piece to an abrupt halt and said with some annoyance, 'My dear Dr Einstein, what's the matter with you? Can't you count?'

*   *   *   *   *

I've Taken a Page in the Bible

An old Jewish man was among the passengers sharing a cramped compartment on a long train journey across country. To make matters worse, it was a baking hot day, and there were no water facilities on the train!

Before the journey was barely an hour old, the old man started: 'Boy! Am I thirsty!'

The first time he said it, the other passengers looked fairly sympathetic. They felt sorry for the old man, but they too were thirsty. It was just one of those things. If there was no water, they would just have to grin and bear it.

But not the old man. Oh, no! He just went on and on: 'Boy! Am I thirsty!'

The other passengers were getting annoyed. And then for what seemed the twentieth time: 'Boy! Am I thirsty!'

Just then, the train pulled into a station. One of the people in the compartment jumped out of his seat, ran down the platform, and returned a few moments later with a large glass of water. 'There you are, old man,' he snapped with barely concealed irritation. The old man thanked him, and drank the water. The train set off, and the passengers settled down to some peace and quiet at last. Before long, the silence was broken:

'Boy!' sighed the old man. 'Was I thirsty!'

*   *   *   *   *

In the year 3036, two men sat in space suits in an airbus between Saturn and Jupiter, returning home from a long day's work. After a while they began to talk.

'What's your name?' asked one.

'Two thousand and seven,' replied the other. 'And yours?'

'Three thousand and eighty-three.'

'Funny, you don't look Jewish!'

*   *   *   *   *

Manny rushed next door to see his friend Joseph one afternoon in a state of great excitement.

'Joseph, it's finished,' he cried.

'What's finished?' asked Joseph.

'Well, you know I said I was going to paint a picture. I've done it, it's finished.'

'OK,' said Joseph, 'let's go and look at it.'

When they got to Manny's house, Joseph was shown the masterpiece. All it consisted of was a canvas covered in blue paint. 'What's it called?' enquired Joseph hesitantly.

'It's called "The Israelites crossing the Red Sea",' announced Manny proudly.

'But I can't see any Israelites.'

'Of course you can't,' said Manny. 'They've crossed already!'

*   *   *   *   *

Fritz Bender wanted to get his girlfriend something special for her birthday, but he didn't have much money. Suddenly, he had an idea. He'd get her a copy of her favourite record, the really romantic one — I suppose you could say it was 'their song'.

So he rang the local record shop — only he was a little careless with his dialling.

'Hello,' said the voice at the other end.

'Hello,' said Fritz. 'I wonder, have you got "A Boy Named Sue"?'

'No,' came the rather bewildered reply, 'but I've got twenty grandchildren in Russia.'

'Is that a record?'

'I don't know about that,' said the voice, 'but in my old village it's above average!'

*   *   *   *   *

I've Taken a Page in the Bible

During the desert campaign in the last war the commander of a small infantry unit called his men together and announced, 'Men, we are not forty miles from El Alamein. We know by our intelligence reports that General Rommel is about to visit a distant unit of the Afrika Korps and can be captured. This is strictly a one-man job. A man disguised as an Arab can capture Rommel. I'd like a volunteer.'

Private Cohen stepped forward. 'Here, sir.'

'Brave man,' said his commanding officer. 'What will you need?'

'All I need, sir, is a radio, supplies and a camel.'

'You shall have them.'

Cohen was away for three months and nothing was heard of him until suddenly a radio message crackled through the news 'Rommel captured'.

There was jubilation throughout all the Allied countries. Newspapers carried the achievement in banner headings.

However, nothing more was heard of Private Cohen or Rommel for months afterwards. Then one day a sentry spotted a little figure staggering across the sand dunes all on his own, dragging a water-bottle and a radio. It was Private Cohen. The moment he arrived in the camp he was taken straight to the senior intelligence officer who asked him, 'Well, where is he?'

'Where's who?'

'Rommel.'

'What do you mean, Rommel?'

'Well, we got your signal "Rommel captured".'

'No, no,' said Private Cohen, 'that should have read, "Camel ruptured".'

*　　*　　*　　*　　*

A small group of soldiers were out on a mission, when it became clear that they were about to confront the enemy.

'This is it, men,' bawled the commander. 'Prepare yourself

200

for some old-fashioned hand-to-hand combat, man against man.'

'Sergeant?'

'Yes, Private Cohen.'

'You know you just said it's going to be man against man.'

'Yes, Cohen, what about it?'

'Well, I was just thinking. If I could be introduced to my man, perhaps we could work things out between ourselves!'

*　　*　　*　　*　　*

A Jew broke his right hand in an accident. The specialist told him that if he wore a cast for five weeks the hand would be as good as new.

'Will I be able to write?' asked the patient.

'Of course,' said the doctor.

'And play the piano?'

'Yes indeed.'

'That's marvellous,' exclaimed the Jew, 'because I couldn't play before!'

*　　*　　*　　*　　*

A Jewish travelling preacher decided to visit his wife only once a year to cut down on costs. Naturally his wife was upset at this and complained to their rabbi.

The preacher came to town and the rabbi sought him out. 'You should visit her at least once a month,' the rabbi said.

'But I can't afford to,' replied the preacher. 'After each visit home my wife has a baby!'

*　　*　　*　　*　　*

*Harpo Marx gives a wonderful example of the convoluted
logic that can seize a Jewish mind when he described an
access of adolescent intelligence in his autobiography*
Harpo Speaks.

At thirteen I attained manhood, according to the Jewish faith. I was *bar mitzvah* — inducted as an adult member of the synagogue. This didn't mean, however, that I would start going to *shul* every Saturday. The rites were performed out of deference to Grandpa, who would have been bitterly hurt if his grandsons hadn't shown this much respect for their traditional faith. It was the least we could do.

For the occasion, Frenchie made me a black serge knee-breeches suit (pieced together of unsold 'lappas') and bought me a derby hat. After the ceremony there was a reception for me at 179 with a spread of sweets, pastries and wine. This, naturally, attracted all the relatives, and it was quite a party. I received four presents. Uncle Al gave me a pair of gloves. Aunt Hannah gave me a pair of gloves. Cousin Sam gave me a pair of gloves. (In my *bar mitzvah* photographs I'm wearing two pairs, one over the other, and holding the third.) Minnie, bless her, gave me a genuine, one-dollar Ingersoll watch.

The inevitable happened. Three days after my *bar mitzvah*, my new watch was missing.

I was pretty damn sore. A present was not the same as something you hustled. I tracked down Chico to a crap game and asked him what about it. He handed me the pawn ticket. I gave the ticket to Minnie and she reclaimed the watch for me. Then a brilliant idea occurred to me. I would show Chico. I would make my watch Chico-proof, so he couldn't possibly hock it again. I removed its hands.

Now the watch was mine forever. I wound it faithfully each
morning and carried it with me at all times. When I wanted
to know what time it was I looked at the Ehret Brewery clock
and held my watch to my ear. It ran like a charm, and its
ticking was a constant reminder that I had, for once,
outsmarted Chico.

In this extract from The Golem, *a story by Avram
Davidson, Mr and Mrs Gumbeiner at home in their
quintessential American home of the early 1930s manage
to carry on a conversation with a total stranger, and between
themselves, without realizing that their uninvited guest is
the Jewish equivalent of Frankenstein. This ability to mis-
understand what is going on and who people are so
comprehensively is a classic example of logical illogicality.
(According to the Talmud the* golem *was the shapeless
mass of Adam's body before God gave it life. In Jewish
folklore the* golem *has developed into a clay model or a
human being brought to life by magic powers, the most
famous being the fabled Golem of Prague, created in the
seventeenth century by Rabbi Judah Lowe to protect the
city's Jews from further persecution.)*

The gray-faced person came along the street where old Mr
and Mrs Gumbeiner lived. It was afternoon, it was
autumn, the sun was warm and soothing to their ancient
bones. Anyone who attended the movies in the twenties or the
early thirties has seen that street a thousand times. Past these
bungalows with their half-double roofs Edmund Lowe
walked arm-in-arm with Leatrice Joy, and Harold Lloyd was
chased by Chinamen waving hatchets. Under these
squamous palm trees Laurel kicked Hardy and Woolsey beat

Wheeler upon the head with codfish. Across these pocket-handkerchief-sized lawns the juveniles of the Our Gang Comedies pursued one another and were pursued by angry fat men in gold knickers. On this same street — or perhaps on some other one of five hundred streets exactly like it.

Mrs Gumbeiner indicated the gray-faced person to her husband.

'You think maybe he's got something the matter?' she asked. 'He walks kind of funny, to me.'

'Walks like a *golem*,' Mr Gumbeiner said indifferently.

The old woman was nettled.

'Oh, I don't know,' she said. 'I think he walks like your cousin Mendel.'

The old man pursed his mouth angrily and chewed on his pipe stem. The gray-faced person turned up the concrete path, walked up the steps to the porch, sat down in a chair. Old Mr Gumbeiner ignored him. His wife stared at the stranger.

'Man comes in without a hello, good-bye, or howareyou, sits himself down and right away he's at home. . . . The chair is comfortable?' she asked. 'Would you like maybe a glass of tea?'

She turned to her husband.

'Say something, Gumbeiner!' she demanded. 'What are you, made of wood?'

The old man smiled a slow, wicked, triumphant smile.

'Why should *I* say something?' he asked the air. 'Who am I? Nothing, that's who.'

The stranger spoke. His voice was harsh and monotonous. 'When you learn who — or rather what — I am, the flesh will melt from your bones in terror.' He bared porcelain teeth.

'Never mind about my bones!' the old woman cried. 'You've got a lot of nerve talking about my bones!'

'You will quake with fear,' said the stranger. Old Mrs Gumbeiner said that she hoped he would live so long. She turned to her husband once again.

'Gumbeiner, when are you going to mow the lawn?'

'All mankind —' the stranger began.

'*Shah!* I'm talking to my husband. . . . He talks *eppis* kind of funny, Gumbeiner, no?'

'Probably a foreigner,' Mr Gumbeiner said, complacently.

'You think so?' Mrs Gumbeiner glanced fleetingly at the stranger. 'He's got a very bad color in his face, *nebbich*. I suppose he came to California for his health.'

'Disease, pain, sorrow, love, grief — all are nought to . . .'

Mr Gumbeiner cut in on the stranger's statement.

'Gall bladder,' the old man said. 'Guinzburg down at the *shule* looked exactly the same before his operation. Two professors they had in for him, and a private nurse day and night.'

'I am not a human being!' the stranger said loudly.

'Three thousand seven hundred and fifty dollars it cost his son, Guinzburg told me. "For you, Poppa, nothing is too expensive — only get well," the son told him.'

'*I am not a human being!*'

'Ai, is that a son for you!' the old woman said, rocking her head. 'A heart of gold, pure gold.' She looked at the stranger. 'All right, all right, I heard you the first time. Gumbeiner! I asked you a question. When are you going to cut the lawn?'

'On Wednesday, *odder* maybe Thursday, comes the Japaneser to the neighborhood. To cut lawns is *his* profession. *My* profession is to be a glazier — retired.'

'Between me and all mankind is an inevitable hatred,' the stranger said. 'When I tell you what I am, the flesh will melt —'

'You said, you said already,' Mr Gumbeiner interrupted.

'In Chicago where the winters were as cold and bitter as the Czar of Russia's heart,' the old woman intoned, 'you had strength to carry the frames with the glass together day in and day out. But in California with the golden sun to mow the lawn when your wife asks, for this you have no strength. Do I call in the Japaneser to cook for you supper?'

'Thirty years Professor Allardyce spent perfecting his theories. Electronics, acuronics —'

'Listen, how educated he talks,' Mr Gumbeiner said, admiringly. 'Maybe he goes to the University here?'

'If he goes to the Unviersity, maybe he knows Bud?' his wife suggested.

'Probably they're in the same class and he came to see him about the homework, no?'

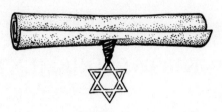

In radio and television there is such a thing as a 'back announcement'. I'd like this to be a back dedication to my late grandmother and grandfather, Booba and Zaide, two wonderful people.

One night I threw a party. All my professional friends were there: actors, solicitors, doctors, and the old couple were sitting in a corner quietly enjoying the company. I think they were getting a little self-conscious that they were not joining in the conversation which was largely about the theatre, when somebody mentioned Charles Dickens. My grandmother saw this as a golden opportunity and chimed in with the comment, 'Oh, Charles Dickens, yes — I saw him last week on a forty-eight bus going to Piccadilly.'

This was followed by a deathly hush over the whole room, and when the party had finished my grandfather took her to one side and said, 'You had to open your big mouth! Alfie was giving such a lovely party, everybody was enjoying themselves, and you had to show your ignorance by opening your big mouth. You saw Charles Dickens on a forty-eight bus going towards Piccadilly? You heard how quiet the room went? No wonder. Since when does a forty-eight bus go to Piccadilly?

ACKNOWLEDGEMENTS

We are grateful for permission to reproduce copyright material from:

Dannie Abse: *A Poet in the Family*, Robson Books.

Sholom Aleichem: *Inside Kasrilevke*, Random House.

Woody Allen: *Without Feathers*, Random House.

Charlotte Chandler: *Hello, I Must be Going: Groucho and his Friends*, Robson Books.

Avram Davidson: 'The Golem' in *The Jewish Caravan*, ed. Leo Schwarz, Holt, Rinehart and Winston.

Montague Glass: *Cousins of Convenience*, William Heinemann. *It's Never Too Late*, William Heinemann.

David Kossoff: *A Small Town is a World*, Robson Books.

Hyam Maccoby: *The Day God Laughed*, Robson Books.

Harpo Marx: *Harpo Speaks*, Robson Books.

Isaac Loebn Peretz: *The Book of Fire*, Thomas Yoselloff, Inc.

Mordecai Richler: *The Apprenticeship of Duddy Kravitz*, André Deutsch.

Maurice Samuel: *The World of Sholom Aleichem*, Alfred Knopf Inc.